The Lost White Race

THE LOST WHITE RACE

By IRA CALVIN

ISBN 978-1-937787-22-6

Published by:

THE BARNES REVIEW
P.O. Box 15877
Washington, D.C. 20003
www.barnesreview.com
1-877-773-9077—toll free ordering line

Copyright 2013 by THE BARNEWS REVIEW. All rights reserved.

Ordering more copies: Order more copies of THE LOST WHITE RACE (softcover, 184 pages, $20 minus 10% for TBR readers plus $5 S&H) from THE BARNES REVIEW, P.O. Box 15877, Washington, D.C. 20003. TBR subscribers may take 10% off the list price. Call TBR toll free at 1-877-773-9077 to charge copies to Visa, MasterCard or Discover. See more products online at www.barnesreview.com.

Subscriptions: A subscription to THE BARNES REVIEW historical magazine is $46 for one year (six issues) and $78 for two years (12 issues) inside the U.S. Outside the U.S: Canada/Mexico: $65 per year. All other nations: $80 per year sent via air mail. Send payment with request to TBR, P.O. Box 15877, Washington, D.C. 20003. Call TBR toll free at 1-877-773-9077 to charge to major credit cards. See also barnesreview.com. See a special subscription offer at the back of this volume or call the toll free number above and ask for best current subscription offer.

Reproduction Policy: Short portions of this book may be reproduced without prior permission in critical reviews and other papers if credit is given to author, full book title is listed and full contact information and subscription information are given for publisher as shown above. No other reproduction of any portion of this book is allowed without permission.

THE LOST WHITE RACE

BY IRA CALVIN

ORIGINALLY PUBLISHED BY
COUNTWAY-WHITE PUBLICATIONS
BROOKLINE, MASSACHUSETTS 1944

2013 EDITION PUBLISHED BY THE BARNES REVIEW

DEDICATION

Dedicated to the white race of the entire world. May that race profit from it, and perpetuate itself 'til Kingdom come.

"The strength of an honest cause is more powerful than any physical weapons mankind has devised or used."

—*David Lawrence*

* * *

"A good book is the precious life-blood of a master spirit, embalmed and treasured up on a purpose to a life beyond life."

—*Milton (Areopagitica)*

* * *

"That writer does the most, who gives his reader the most knowledge, and takes from him the least time."

—*C.C. Colton*

* * *

"The language of truth is unadorned and always simple."

—*Ammianus Marcelinus*

* * *

"Neither cast ye your pearls before swine, lest they trample them under their feet."

—*Matthew VII: 6*

* * *

"To lay aside all prejudices is to lay aside all principles. He who is destitute of principles is governed by whims."

—*F. Jacobi*

* * *

"Every man has an inalienable right to express his opinion, and any man who would deny another this right is sanctioning a principle upon which he himself may later be forbidden to speak or write his own."

—*Not with apologies, but thanks, to Thomas Paine; the man whose writings inspired this book. May the libraries of the world forever keep his literary works in circulation.*

Table of Contents

INTRODUCTION: All Is Not Lost 7

FOREWORD: Dashed to Destruction? 9

PREFACE: The Salvation of Mankind 11

CHAPTER ONE: Our Great Domestic Problem 19

CHAPTER TWO: The Illusion That Exclusion Is Abuse 71

CHAPTER THREE: Why So Many Races of People? 79

CHAPTER FOUR: CIvilization Versus Barbarism 96

CHAPTER FIVE: Our Deluded Leaders 107

CHAPTER SIX: Newspaper Clippings & Comments 115

CHAPTER SEVEN: Can We Plan Our Civilization? 151

CHAPTER EIGHT: A Separate State for the Negro 167

CHAPTER NINE: Preventing Extinction 175

White folk have built the vast majority of the greatest monuments created by man. Pictured is Amiens Cathedral in France, one of hundreds of inspiring cathedrals built by whites during the Middle Ages.

INTRODUCTION

All Is Not Lost

White folks, here is your "second bible." *The Lost White Race,* by Ira Calvin. At the time the book was first published in 1944, Calvin was a soldier serving in the U.S. military in the Pacific War against Japan. Thus, this book is a product of its time and offers a fascinating, if antiquated, insight into racial politics in America during the mid-20th century. Although stridently pro-segregation, the author did however accept that this policy was ultimately immoral, and that the only fair solution to the racial problem was geographical physical separation. Calvin takes the stand that, "as long as we are going to set the world in order, we might just as well decide right now that there will have be two worlds, i.e., a white world and a colored world." He maintained that if we did not do this, the white race would eventually be dissolved, and in the end there would be only one world: a colored one.

Calvin pulled no punches against what he called "colored" folks—Japanese and other East Asians, other non-whites and especially negroes. He proposed appropriate measures for preserving the endangered white race before too late. He denounced in no uncertain terms the forced mingling of the white and negro races—which has only gotten worse in the following half-century. His wisdom will doubtless find many followers among the disgruntled and dispossessed whites of the 21st century.

Careful readers will note that Calvin includes Jews among the white race. You must bear in mind that genetics in 1944 was still in its infancy. The title of the book is unfortunate as it sounds either downbeat, as in "all is lost," or resistance is useless, or else as if the book were about Atlantis or Kennewick Man or the like. It is not. It is an insightful essay on morality, civilization and how the white race can still be saved, and will prove useful in the coming decades and centuries.

—JOHN TIFFANY
Assistant Editor
THE BARNES REVIEW

FOREWORD

Dashed to Destruction?

In writing this book, I feel like a man who is standing on a peaceful cliff looking down on a raging torrent, knowing that he must plunge into it to save a drowning child, yet aware of the possibility that both he and the child may be dashed to destruction and death before the rapids are cleared. But my duty is clear to me, and it shall not be said that I cared more for my personal safety than I did for the life of that beautiful, innocent child. I shall take the child over those terrible rapids, and even though I am battered to pieces when we reach the calm waters below, she must still be the same lovely little girl she always was ... for in her resides the whole future white race.

Now I find myself "casting one last longing, lingering look behind" at that "cool, sequestered vale of life" to which I have always been accustomed, and to which all private citizens have a right in time of peace, but not in time of war. ... But I must not tarry here ... the child is drowning ... so here I go overboard, and may the Almighty God be with me.

—THE AUTHOR

Long before the Egyptians were starting construction on the pyramids, ancient whites were in the midst of planning and building Stonehenge, one of literally thousands of massive, astronomically aligned megalithic structures across Europe.

PREFACE

The Salvation of Mankind

In this book I have attempted to put into words what at least 80,000,000 good, decent Americans are thinking; and to clarify that thinking, which of late has become dangerously confused from reading and listening to the opinions of a small body of articulate persons; persons who, whatever their motives, are completely at variance with solid American ideals.

I believe that the home and family are the salvation of mankind ... that the pride a man takes in his home and his wife and children is the one thing that keeps him civilized; makes him shave every day, wear decent clothes, behave himself in public, try to improve himself, and obey the law. This moral and civilized behavior of the married man influences the unmarried man, and forces him to behave likewise, or be considered a barbarian.

We must maintain our national pride in the family if we are to continue as a strong Nation. That some persons among us have been trying to destroy that pride is one thing I have made an effort to show.

Civilization, as we know it, is based on the family, and if the family goes, civilization goes with it. The whole thing is based on pride, and if pride is destroyed, everything is destroyed. The white race would not be in existence today if it had not been proud of its distinctive, white, translucent skin. But we have a natural pride of race, which is the solid rock foundation on which rest all of our other lesser prides.

As the whole structure depends on the foundation for its support, we must not permit that foundation to be wrecked.

There are really only two families in the world: i.e., the white family, and the colored family. When we reflect on the matter, we can easily see that such a division of the peoples of the world is the only sensible way to settle the race question. Now, the colored family will have to be made to understand that our family's continued existence depends on our not permitting the members of the two families to mix socially. Since the continued existence of the white family requires that members of the colored family be excluded from it, one cannot blame the white family for enforcing that exclusion. The great colored family of the world has no more right to demand to be admitted into the great white family of the world than a private colored family has to demand to be admitted into the sacred precincts of a private white family.

In either case the destruction of the white family would be as certain as that the oncoming night gradually obliterates the light of day.

The Japanese have glaringly demonstrated that the white race will either have to hold the upper hand in this world, or be exterminated.

The fight we are having with Germany is really a fight within our own family. Since records have been kept, families have been known to fight among themselves, but when any outside family attacked either, the families warring among themselves stopped their quarrel long enough to join in battling off the strange invader. When two white peoples go to war, neither is obliterated, no matter which wins, and as no white people have ever been held in slavery for any length of time, that fear is of little consequence. The reason for this is that the white men held in slavery would have just as beautiful daughters as the slave masters, and since women can determine the courses of empires, the daughters of the enslaved would soon get them released. If there is any instance in the history of mankind where a colored race held a white people in slavery, I do not know about it. If it has happened, and the white people were not rescued in a short time, they must have simply disappeared.

There is one instance I know of, and practically every white American knows of it; it is the story of the Lost Colony of Roanoke. Sir Walter Raleigh sent this colony to settle on the island of Roanoke off the coast of Virginia and North Carolina. There were about one hundred and fifty men, women and children in the party, which was headed by Governor John White. The governor's daughter, Eleanor White, was with them. She was the wife of Ananias Dare, one of Governor White's assistants.

To her was born the first white child of the New World, soon after they landed. They named her Virginia, after the name Governor White had given the country. North Carolina has named the County in which Roanoke is situated Dare, in her honor.

When Virginia was about one week old, Governor White decided to take their one little ship and sail back to England for help and supplies, as a previous expedition which had plenty of supplies had been completely wiped out by the Indians, and the supplies they expected to find destroyed. When Governor White landed in England the Spanish War had broken out and he was unable to get back to Roanoke until three years later. And what did he find?

The island was deserted. There were no signs of human life.

Apparently the Indians had murdered all the men, and probably some of the women and children. The only evidence we have today that they did not murder all the white women and female children is the red hair and grey eyes of some of the Croatan Indians in North Carolina.

One thing which I wish to impress on the reader of this book is that I do not have any hatred for, and do not sanction any hatred of, any colored race of people on this Earth. But at the same time, I profess to love my own race—the white race—with my whole heart, and desire to see it on the road to being preserved for all time before I depart this life. The white race must become united into one great family if it is to survive. It must not keep on killing off thousands of its own members in unnecessary wars. It delights the tiger in the bush to see two handsome bucks wearing each other down in a fight to the death. He smiles as he licks his chops, knowing that the victor will be so weakened he will be easy prey for the kill. They fight each other—he gets both.

This is no time for silence, for silence now means the death of the white race. This is a time for plain talk. Since our young people are being taught everything they should not learn, it behooves us to teach them a few things which they will realize later was for their own survival. If powerful Negro organizations have the freedom of our press to tell our children that they are no better than Negroes, we ought to have the freedom of that same press to fight back for our own preservation.

Every one of us has had it instilled into us to be modest and not to boast of being prettier or brighter than another, but it looks now as if we were going to have to drop this false modesty and proclaim to the world that we think our own children are the prettiest in the world, and that their white skin is worth saving.

This book properly labels those who are traitors to their own race, and from now on they can come out into the open and declare themselves. They cannot plead ignorance. They know what they are doing, and the world knows what they are doing, which is more important. We want no more of this foolishness of people in a small town in the North who have only one or two Negro families living therein, proclaiming themselves experts on the Negro question. They do not know that those few Negroes behave because they know what is good for them, and that underneath those black smiles there lurks a determination to get on top, and do the looking down themselves.

You hear much talk of love of country, and also much talk of one race of men being as good as another. Your race makes your country what it is, and therefore, if you love your country you must love even more your race which makes it what it is. The United States would not be such a great country to live in if it were populated by any race other than the White. When you speak of country you do not mean the land merely, but of the people who populate that land. The white race could take over any country and remake it into a country like our own.

Let no man say that what I have written in this book will cause the Negroes to desert us in this war. The Negro knows that we treat him better than any other people would treat him, and that we shall continue to protect and even feed him if necessary. However, we are not going to take a fatal step which would lead to the extermination of the white race, and as a consequence, the end of civilization.

I have made a rather extensive study of Abraham Lincoln's speeches and writings in order that I might know for myself just how he felt about the social equality of Negroes with white people, and I have been greatly enlightened. As the reader will learn from the quotations from his life, he wanted only freedom for the Negroes, and not social equality, as he clearly saw the disaster which would befall the white race if such be attempted. Any white man will agree that we do not want to either enslave the Negro or persecute him. We only want to preserve the white race.

Some people will say that I am shouting "fire," and President Roosevelt has said that it might be considered a crime to shout "fire" in a crowded theater when there is no fire, but let's consider that there is a fire, would it not be an equal crime to not shout "fire" if you were the only person who saw it, and the house was in fact in flames?

Well, I maintain that there is not only a fire, but a conflagration, which will consume us if we do not come out of this drugged sleep, and set out to fight this fire with fire. My father taught me when I was very young that it is permissible to light one fire against the wind to meet the forest fire coming toward your house which will destroy it and everything else unless it is kept away. Many a time have I thrilled at seeing our back-fire against the wind, as slow as it was, finally meet the raging fire and snuff it out as if it were no raging monster at all.

Now I am fighting a different kind of fire, but it is a fact that this fire requires a fire to meet it, and here it is. This book is not written merely for this generation, but in case that this generation does not solve this problem, it is written for the next generation, and the next, and so on, until it is solved.

Bear this in mind, when you look on with placid eye, at a Negro living with a white girl, you are advocating and sanctioning the downfall of the white race, which means the disappearance from this Earth of blue eyes, blond hair, and lovely pink skin. Do you need proof of this?

Then look closely at the next mulatto you come into close contact with and check on the named "things of beauty." You will not find any one of them. Even the ears have a death-like yellowness. Just check—I ask you!

There will be those who will say that we ought not to talk about this subject, and if there is any man who detests the whole subject any more than I do I would like to meet him, but the Negroes themselves have caused this by their battle to get into our society. If we saw a fire coming toward our house which will surely destroy it, it would be the height of folly to keep quiet about it. Take another case: A man is sitting quietly in his house reading a magazine, and suddenly four men burst into the house bent upon ravishing his pretty daughters, would we expect him to sit still and declare that as far as he is concerned he is a pacifist, and will offer no fight?

And about the Negroes helping us in this war. If you desire to get a man to help you do something, there is a limit to what you will be willing to pay for that help. As for me I declare for being fair in all things. To let the Negro believe, and encourage him to believe, that we are willing to sacrifice our very existence in order to get him to go along and help us win this war is a crime on our part. He should never have been led to believe such a foolish thing as that. We are supposed to be fighting to preserve our liberty, and one might ask—what liberty— the liberty to destroy ourselves by permitting the Negroes to enter our society and utterly destroy all white people?

Heretofore, in our Country the white people have had the liberty to—as Lincoln said—"just let the Negroes alone" but things have taken a dangerous turn, of late, and our Government has been trying to force white people to accept them into their company whether they could do that safely or not. Is that the kind of liberty we are fighting for? It has come to the point where the Negroes do not want to be left to their own devices, but want to butt into the white man's affairs. Nothing good can come of this, and they ought to take warning and start building up a world of their own.

Even though I have had to point out, for emphasis, certain serious mistakes that President and Mrs. Roosevelt, Harold Ickes, and Vice-President Wallace, have made, I feel that they, being our best people, will take it as with the best of intentions for the future welfare of our family, and forgive me, for I would do no one any harm, and only desire to bring us out of this dreamless sleep of death.

When a man sees a job like this that needs doing, he has to put the welfare of his people above his own best interests, and in this connection Thomas Gray expresses my thoughts beautifully in these three lines:

> The threats of pain and ruin to despise,
>   To scatter plenty o'er a smiling land,
>   And read their history in a nation's (blue) eyes.

I had been wanting to write this book for quite a long time, but was at a loss as just how to get started, so I began haunting the libraries, and lo and behold! I found that our grand ancestors had already written it for me, and I realized that their souls were crying to me from the tomb to get busy and set the world right on what they had said and written on the subject. So I want to offer up my thanks to them, and also express my sincere gratitude to Providence for being on beauty's side . . . for beauty and brains do go together. Think for a moment of the fact that you have never seen a really beautiful insane person. Also reflect a little on how the Almighty keeps the brains of the white race a step or two ahead of the colored race. There must be celestial design in all this.

CHAPTER ONE

Our Great Domestic Problem

Rebellion against destruction is obedience to God.

A family had an eagle for a pet, and he had been trained to act the gentleman. They liked to watch him walking majestically around the yard. He was a powerful bird, but became ill, and one day while he was recuperating they left the door of his cage open. A rooster from next door, known for being a troublemaker, walked into the yard, spied the eagle, and went for him. The eagle was at a loss to know what the rooster was trying to do to him. Then it dawned upon him that he was being attacked. He drew himself up in all his dignity, reached out with one mighty talon, took the rooster by the neck, stepped on his back with his other claw, and pulled his head off.

That should be a good moral lesson to minority groups in these United States who are constantly irritating and annoying that great majority, the real, honest American people. These minority groups are not content to be let alone. They want the majority to accept their laws and regulations, which they cook up for their exclusive benefit. The majority have been sick, as it were; unorganized, and not aware that they were being attacked. But now one can sense a stir of action coming.

Under the false cloak of democracy these minority groups have just about demoralized this whole Nation. By the press, by the radio, and even by school books, they have been trying to destroy pride of ancestry, because they themselves have no ancestry to be proud of. It is amazing how many intelligent, educated people have allowed themselves to fall under the influence of this pride-destroying barrage of spurious literature. Why, it has some otherwise sensible people believing that black is white!

Yes, taking advantage of the freedom which democracy gives, they have written and published books which no decent white man would permit in his house, or in the public libraries even, if he knew about them. One of the more recent of these books is written by Richard Wright, and is a pack of lies, disguised under a thin screen of fiction. It is along the lines of *Uncle Tom's Cabin*, and is entitled *Uncle Tom's Children*. This Wright has the nerve to picture Southern white men as brutal perverts who go about chasing Negro wenches, and Southern white women as not being morally fit for even Negro men to associate with. Wright, of course, is a Negro himself. The short tales he tells in this book are out-and-out lies, designed to stir up sympathy among honest people who do not know, and cannot know, the actual truth. He plays on the spilling of blood, by himself, under the whip and lash of Southern white men. Anyone who knows anything about Southern white men will tell you that they are gentle and kind and would not hurt a mouse unless attacked. The whole trouble is that they have been too gentle and kind. That is all over now.

How this Wright can be allowed to write and publish a book which on the face of it is filthy and degrading, at this crucial time when everyone is crying for unity, is beyond comprehension. Any white man who reads that book and does not feel justifiable indignation is a swine of the lowest order. What right have Negroes to hold white women up to criticism? In this case the right to ridicule is tantamount to the right to destroy, and are we going to let them destroy our women? The lowest kind of white men and women can still produce beautiful children, and the highest grade Negroes cannot do that. God willed it so, and it is up to the white man to see that His will is carried out. You can't get around the truth that a Negro is certain death to blue eyes, blonde hair, and pink, translucent skin.

The colored man, be he Japanese, Chinese, Indian, or Negro, is the natural enemy of the white man, in the same way that the tiger is the natural enemy of the lamb. If the lamb permits himself to become too friendly with the tiger, we all know what will become of him . . . he will become incorporated into the tiger, and no trace of him will be left. The tiger will not become less vicious for having absorbed the lamb, nor would the tiger take on any one of the lamb's good qualities.

The lamb would have served no other good purpose than that momentary enjoyment the tiger received in the eating of him.

The same is true as far as the white race is concerned . . . it could become too friendly with the colored race, and in time would be absorbed by that race, and disappear entirely. And what good would that do the world? The yellow resulting race would not be any better than the Japanese are at this day. Civilization would be at an end, and the fate of mankind the rubbish heap.

It might be well to point out right here that the incontrovertible fact that the colored man is the natural enemy of the white man, is not the fault of the white man. God made the tiger the enemy of the lamb, and in the present case the colored man the certain destroyer of the white man, and the white man had nothing to do with this arrangement.

He only found out this state of affairs by use of the faculties which God endowed him with . . . his mind and his eyes. Why God made white women beautiful like His own angels, and gave white men eyes with which to recognize this fact, and then created other women not lovely to white men's eyes, is a matter we need not take up here.

Now let us view the relation of the white man to the colored man from an entirely different angle. Every adult who is in his right mind knows that the good and beautiful things in this world are rather delicate, and can easily be destroyed by the more vigorous and less useful things. Take the rose, for instance; it is beautiful but delicate, and if you do not keep the weeds, (which are more vigorous and will take over any garden if not kept down) away from it they will choke it to death in time. All pretty flowers have to be nursed and cared for or they will not long survive the onslaught of the homely, but persistent weeds.

If you ask me why God made our field and garden-grown fruits and vegetables less vigorous than useless bushes and weeds, and makes us sweat even to eat, I cannot tell you . . . I only know that such is a fact which cannot be refuted. Anyway, He endowed us with the brains to see what to do and how to do it. We can be thankful for that.

And this is what I am driving at. The white race is the most beautiful race of men and women on Earth . . . and like the flowers and vegetables, the most easily destroyed. It can be destroyed even if it fights destruction, but it can be much more easily destroyed if it does not fight for survival. The Negro here among us now can be considered as weeds which are determined to out-produce us, out-vote us, and in the end destroy us. You'll find these weeds right now creeping into our legislative halls, and attempting to get legislation put into effect which would give them a better strangle-hold upon us. Let's get rid of the weeds; before they get rid of us.

Up until now, men and women guilty of acts which would lead to the destruction of the white race could plead that they did not know such acts might lead to so dire a result. It is entirely possible, for instance, that Margaret Webster, who produced Othello, or Uta Hagen, who played the wife of the Negro, Paul Robeson, did not know that they were setting a dangerous example for our young girls. My good mother used to quote this truth to me:

> Vice is a monster of such frightful mien
>   That to be hated, needs but to be seen,
>   But seen too oft, familiar with her face,
>   We first endure, then pity, then embrace!
> —POPE

Or Mrs. Roosevelt may not have known, when she said that a person's choice of a marriage partner was his or her own affair, and concerned nobody else, that she was leading our young folks to believe that their family was nothing to them . . . that they could disgrace their own family with impunity if they chose to do so. Thank heavens, the children think more of their parents than that, and thank heavens again, that the parents let the children know in no uncertain terms, that if they go over the color line they are done with them forever.

According to the *Negro Year Book*, 1937-1938, the population of the Earth consisted of the following races:

White	827,000,000
Yellow	870,000,000
Black	302,000,000
Total	1,999,000,000

Now, it will be seen from the above figures that the yellow race, which is a colored race, the same as the Negro, outnumbers the white race by over 40,000,000. Add the Negro population of the world to the plurality held by the yellow race and you will find that the combined colored race outnumbers the white by 345,000,000.

What does this mean?

It means that the white race of the world is already in the minority, and is on the defensive, but does not know it. The white man is supposed to have the advantage in brains, but right now he certainly is not showing it. Indeed, he is practically in the process of voting himself out of existence. Since the insane John Brown slaughtered sleeping, helpless, innocent people in the territory of Kansas, just prior to the Civil War, and later made a suicidal raid on Harper's Ferry, there has existed a serious and dangerous situation in this country.

After this Nation had been drenched in blood in the most futile war that has ever been waged on this Earth, and the great Lincoln was trying to bring order out of chaos, a man with a club foot and warped mind, Thaddeus Stevens, got control of the Congress and made it do his bidding. He was the Congress, for no man in that Congress dared defy him. He forced laws through that put the great people of the South under the rule of the Negroes. It was his announced intention to Africanize the people. Revenge was what he wanted. At the time, he was under the evil influence of a Negress with an animal-like beauty, who was apparently his mistress, and dictated his policies. Later, when he saw his plans collapsing, and realized that Negroes cannot rule white people for long, he admitted that, having sunk so low himself, he had hoped to redeem his respectability by dragging millions of white people down to his own level. He became very ill in the midst of his nefarious scheme, and one could think that the mighty hand of God struck him low so that he could not further degrade a great people. He lived long enough to see that people, ground into the dust by the oppressor, create an invisible empire, which challenged the monstrous visible empire to mortal combat, and won.

Ever since Abraham Lincoln has been dead he has been quoted and misquoted, mostly misquoted; especially about what he had to say in regard to all men being created equal. People lift out one sentence, or part of a sentence, from another person's speech or writings, and it does not tell what that person meant to say. Worse still, it is often held out to mean just the opposite from what was intended. Now, I am going to quote you Mr. Lincoln's exact words on what he thought about the African race. You'll be surprised! Why? Well, because you know, and I know, that the Negroes are basing their whole fight for equality with white people on that little misquote "all men are created equal."

September 16, 1859—Speech at COLUMBUS, OHIO

In the first pitched battle which Senator Douglas and myself had, at the town of Ottawa, I used the language which I will now read. Having been previously reading an extract, I continued as follows:

"Now, gentlemen, I don't want to read at any greater length, but this is the true complexion of all I have ever said in regard to the institution of slavery and the black race. This is the whole of it, and anything that argues me into his idea of perfect social and political equality with the Negro is but a specious and fantastic arrangement of words, by which a man can prove a horse-chestnut to be a chestnut horse. I will say here, while upon this subject, that I have no purpose either directly or indirectly to interfere with the institution of slavery in the States where it exists. I believe I have no lawful right to do so, and I have no inclination to do so.

"I have no purpose to introduce political and social equality between the white and black races. There is a physical difference between the two which, in my judgment, will forever forbid their living together upon the footing of perfect equality, and inasmuch as it becomes a necessity that there must be a difference, I, as well as Judge Douglas, am in favor of the race to which I belong having the superior position. I have never said anything to the contrary, but

I hold that, notwithstanding all this, there is no reason in the world why the Negro is not entitled to all the natural rights enumerated in the Declaration of Independence, the right to life, liberty, and the pursuit of happiness. I hold that he is as much entitled to these as the white man. I agree with Judge Douglas, he is not my equal in many respects—certainly not in color, perhaps not in moral or intellectual endowments. But in the right to eat the bread, without leave of anybody else, which his own hand earns, he is my equal, and the equal of Judge Douglas, and the equal of every living man.

"Upon a subsequent occasion, when the reason for making a statement like this recurred, I said:

"While I was at the hotel today an elderly gentleman called upon me to know whether I was really in favor of producing a perfect equality between the Negroes and white people. While I had not proposed to myself on this occasion to say much on that subject, yet as the question was asked me I thought I would occupy perhaps five minutes in saying something in regard to it. I will say, then, that I am not, nor ever have been, in favor of bringing about in any way the social and political equality of the white and black races—that I am not, nor ever have been, in favor of making voters or jurors of the Negroes, nor of qualifying them to hold office, nor to intermarry with the white people; and I will say in addition to this, that there is a physical difference between the black and the white races, which, I believe, will forever forbid the two races living together on terms of social and political equality. And inasmuch as they cannot so live, while they do remain together there must be the position, of superior and inferior, and I, as much as any other man, am in favor of having the superior position assigned to the white race. I say upon this occasion I do not perceive that because the white man is to have the superior position, the Negro should be denied everything. I do not understand that because I do not want a Negro woman for a slave, I must necessarily want one for a wife. My understanding is that I can just let her alone. I am now in my fiftieth year; and I certainly never have had a black woman for either a slave or a wife.

"So it seems to me quite possible for us to get along without making either slaves or wives of the Negroes. I will add to this, that I have never seen to my knowledge a man, woman or child who was in favor of producing a perfect equality, social and political, between Negroes and white men. I recollect but one distinguished instance that I ever heard of so frequently as to be entirely satisfied of its correctness—and that is the case of Judge Douglas' old friend, Colonel Richard M. Johnson. I will also add to the remarks I have made (for I am not going to enter at large upon this subject), that I have never had the least apprehension that I or my friends would marry Negroes, if there was no law to keep them from it; but as Judge Douglas and his friends seem to be in great apprehension that they might, if there were no law to keep them from it, I give him my most solemn pledge that I will to the very last stand by the law of the State, which forbids the marrying of white people with Negroes.

"There, my friends, you have briefly what I have, upon former occasions, said upon the subject to which this newspaper, to the extent of its ability, has drawn public attention. In it you not only perceive, as a probability, that in that contest I did not at any time say I was in favour of Negro suffrage; but the absolute proof that twice—once substantially and once expressly—I declared against it. Having shown you this, there remains but a word of comment upon that newspaper article. It is this: that I presume the editor of that paper is an honest and truth-loving man, and that he will be greatly obliged to me for furnishing him thus early an opportunity to correct the misrepresentation he has made, before it has run so long that malicious people can call him a liar."

                    End of first quote.

Now here is part of a speech made September 17, 1859, at Cincinnati, Ohio:

"My fellow-citizens of the State of Ohio: This is the first time in my life that I have appeared before an audience in so great a city as this. I therefore—though I am no longer a young man—make this appearance under some degree of embarrassment. But I have found that when one is embarrassed, usually the shortest way to get through with it is to quit thinking or talking about it, and go at something else.

"I understand that you have had recently with you my very distinguished friend, Judge Douglas, of Illinois, and I understand, without having had an opportunity (not greatly sought to be sure) of seeing a report of the speech that he made here, that he did me the honor to mention my humble name. I suppose that he did so for the purpose of making some objection to some sentiment at some time expressed by me. I should expect, it is true, that Judge Douglas had reminded you, or informed you, if you had never before heard of it, that I had once in my life declared it as my opinion that this government cannot "endure permanently half slave and half free; that a house divided against itself cannot stand," and, as I had expressed it, I did not expect the house to fall; that I did not expect the Union to be dissolved, but that I did expect it would cease to be divided; that it would become all one thing or all the other; that either the opposition of slavery will arrest the further spread of it, and place it where the public mind would rest in the belief that it was in the course of ultimate extinction, or the friends of slavery will push forward until it becomes alike lawful in all the States, old or new, free as well as slave. I did, fifteen months ago, express that opinion, and upon many occasions Judge Douglas has denounced it, and has greatly, intentionally or unintentionally, misrepresented my purpose in the expression of that opinion. I presume, without having seen a report of his speech, that he did so here. I presume that he alluded also to that opinion in different language, having been expressed at a subsequent time by Governor Seward, of New York, and that he took the two in a lump and denounced them; that he tried to point out that there was something couched in this opinion which led to the making of an entire uniformity of the local institutions of the various States of the Union, in utter disregard of the different States, which in their nature would seem to require a variety of institutions, and a variety of laws conforming to the differences in the nature of the different States.

"This charge, in this form, was made by Judge Douglas on, I believe, the 9th of July, 1858, in Chicago, in my hearing. On the next evening, I made some reply to it. I informed him that many of the inferences he drew from that expression of mine were altogether foreign to any purpose entertained by me, and in so far as he should ascribe these inferences to me, as my purpose, he was entirely mistaken; and in so far as he might argue that whatever might be my purpose, actions, conforming to my views, would lead to these results, he might argue and establish if he could; but so far as purposes were concerned, he was totally mistaken as to me.

"When I made that reply to him, I told him, on the question of declaring war between the different States of the Union, that I had not said I did not expect any peace upon this question until slavery was exterminated; that I had only said I expected peace when that institution was put where the public mind should rest in the belief that it was in course of ultimate extinction; that I believed, from the organization of our government until a very recent period of time, the institution had been placed and continued upon such a basis; that we had had comparative peace upon that question through a portion of that period of time, only because the public mind rested in that belief in regard to it, and that when we returned to that position in relation to that matter, I supposed we should again have peace as we previously had. I assured him, as I now assure you, that I neither then had, nor have, nor ever had, any purpose in any way of interfering with the institution of slavery where it exists. I believe we have no power, under the Constitution of the United States, or rather under the form of government under which we live, to interfere with the institution of slavery, or any other of the institutions of our sister States. I declared then, and I now re-declare, that I have as little inclination to interfere with the institution of slavery where it now exists, through the instrumentality of the General Government, or any other instrumentality, as I believe we have no power to do so. I accidently used this expression: I had no purpose of entering into the slave States to disturb the institution of slavery. So, upon the first occasion that Judge Douglas got an opportunity to reply to me, he passed by the whole body of what I had said upon the subject, and seized upon that particular expression of mine, that I had no purpose of entering into the slave States to disturb the institution of slavery.

"'Oh, no,' said he; 'he (Lincoln) won't enter into the slave States to disturb the institution of slavery; he is too prudent a man to do that; he only means that he will go on to the line between the free and the slave States, and shoot over at them. This is all he means to do. He means to do them all the harm he can, to disturb them all he can, in such a way as to keep his own hide in perfect safety.'

"Well, now, I did not think, at the time, that that was either a very dignified or very logical argument; but so it was, and I had to get along with it as well as I could.

"It has occurred to me here tonight that if I ever do shoot over the line at the people on the other side of the line, into a slave State, and propose to do so, keeping my own skin safe, that I have now about the best chance I shall ever have. I should not wonder if there are some Kentuckians about this audience; we are close to Kentucky; and whether that be so or not, we are on elevated ground, and by speaking distinctly I should not wonder if some of the Kentuckians would hear me on the other side of the river. For that reason I propose to address a portion of what I say to the Kentuckians.

"I say, then, in the first place, to the Kentuckians, that I am what they call, as I understand it, a "Black Republican." I think slavery is wrong, morally and politically. I desire that it should be no further spread in these United States, and I should not object if it should gradually terminate in this whole Union. While I say this for myself, I say to you Kentuckians that I understand you differ radically with me upon this proposition; that you believe slavery is a good thing; that slavery is right; that it ought to be extended and perpetuated in this Union. Now, there being this broad difference between us, I do not pretend, in addressing myself to you Kentuckians, to attempt proselyting (converting) you; that would be a vain effort. I do not enter upon it. I only propose to try to show you that you ought to nominate for the next presidency, at Charleston, my distinguished friend, Judge Douglas. In all that there is no real difference between you and him; I understand he is as sincerely for you, and more wisely for you, than you are for yourselves. I will try to demonstrate that proposition. Understand now, I say that I believe he is as sincerely for you, and more wisely for you, than you are yourselves.

"What do you want more than anything else to make successful your views of slavery—to advance the outspread of it, and to secure and perpetuate the nationality of it? What is needed absolutely? What is indispensable to you? Why, if I may be allowed to answer the question, it is to retain a hold upon the North—it is to retain support and strength from the free States. If you can get this support and strength from the free States, you can succeed. If you do not get this support and this strength from the free States, you are in the minority, and you are beaten at once. (Writer's note: Minorities take note.)

"If that proposition is admitted—and it is undeniable—then the next thing I say to you is, that Douglas of all the men in this nation is the only man that affords you any hold upon the free States; that no other man can give you any strength in the free States. This being so, if you doubt the other branch of the proposition, whether he is for you—whether he really is for you, as I have expressed it—I propose asking your attention for a while to a few facts.

"The issue between you and me, understand, is that I think slavery is wrong, and ought not to be outspread, and you think it is right, and ought to be extended and perpetuated. I now proceed to try to show you that Douglas is as sincerely for you, and more wisely for you, than you are for yourselves.

"In the first place, we know that in a government like this, a government of the people, where the voice of all men of the country, substantially, enters into the administration of the government, what lies at the bottom of all of it is public opinion. I lay down the proposition that Judge Douglas is not only the man that promises you in advance a hold upon the North, and support in the North, but that he constantly molds public opinion to your ends; that in every possible way he can, he molds the public opinion of the North to your ends; and if there are a few things which he says that appear to be against you, and a few that he forbears to say which you would like to have him say—you ought to remember that the saying of the one, or the forbearing to say the other, would lose his hold upon the North, and, by consequence, would lose his capacity to serve you.

"Upon this subject of molding public opinion, I call your attention to the fact—for a well-established fact it is—that the Judge never says your institution of slavery is wrong. There is not a public man in the United States, I believe, with the exception of Senator Douglas, who has not, at some time in his life, declared his opinion whether the thing is right or wrong; but Senator Douglas never declares it is wrong. He leaves himself at perfect liberty to do all in your favor which he would be hindered from doing if he were to declare the thing to be wrong. On the contrary, he takes all the chances that he has for inveigling the sentiment of the North, opposed to slavery, into your support, by never saying it is right. This you ought to set down to his credit. You ought to give him full credit for this much, little though it be in comparison to the whole which he does for you.

"Some other things I will ask your attention to. He said upon the floor of the United States Senate, and he has repeated it, as I understand, a great many times, that he does not care whether slavery is "voted up or voted down." This again shows you, or ought to show you, if you reason upon it, that he does not believe it to be wrong; for a man may say, when he sees nothing wrong in a thing, that he does not care whether it be voted up or voted down; but no man can logically say that he cares not whether a thing goes up or goes down which appears to him to be wrong. You therefore have a demonstration in this, that to Judge Douglas' mind your favorite institution, which you desire to have spread out and made perpetual, is no wrong.

"Another thing he tells you, in a speech made at Memphis, in Tennessee, shortly after the canvass in Illinois, last year. He there distinctly told the people that there was a "line drawn by the Almighty across this continent, on the one side of which the soil must always be cultivated by slaves"; that he did not pretend to know exactly where that line was, but that there was such a line. I want to ask your attention to that proposition again—that there is one portion of this continent where the Almighty has designed the soil shall always be cultivated by slaves; that its being cultivated by slaves at that place is right; that it has the direct sympathy and the authority of the Almighty. Whenever you can get these Northern audiences to adopt the opinion that slavery is right on the other side of the Ohio; whenever you can get them, in pursuance of Douglas' views, to adopt that sentiment, they will readily make the other argument, which is perfectly logical, that that which is right on that side of the Ohio cannot be wrong on this, and that if you have that property on that side of the Ohio, under the seal and stamp of the Almighty, when by any means it escapes over here, it is wrong to have constitutions and laws "to devil" you about it. So Douglas is molding public opinion in the North, first to say that the thing is right in your State over the Ohio River, and hence to say that that which is right there is not wrong here, and that all laws and constitutions here, recognizing it as being wrong, are themselves wrong, and ought to be repealed and abrogated. He will tell you, men of Ohio, that if you choose here to have laws against slavery, it is in conformity to the idea that your climate is not suited to it; that your climate is not suited to slave labor, and therefore you have constitutions and laws against it.

"Let us attend to that argument for a little while, and see if it be sound. You do not raise sugar-cane (except the new-fashioned sugar-cane, and you won't raise that long), but they do raise it in Louisiana. You don't raise it in Ohio because you can't raise it profitably, because the climate don't suit it. They do raise it in Louisiana because there it is profitable.

Now Douglas will tell you that is precisely the slavery question: that they do have slaves there because they are profitable, and you don't have them here because they are not profitable. If that is so, then it leads to dealing with the one precisely as with the other. Is there, then, anything in the constitution or laws of Ohio against raising sugar-cane? Have you found it necessary to put any such provision in your law? Surely not! No man desires to raise sugar-cane in Ohio; but if any man did desire to do so, you would say that it was a tyrannical law that forbids his doing so; and whenever you shall agree with Douglas, whenever your minds are brought to adopt his argument, as surely will you have reached the conclusion that although slavery is not profitable in Ohio, if any man want it, it is a wrong to him not to let him have it.

"In this matter Judge Douglas is preparing the public mind for you in Kentucky, to make perpetual that good thing in your estimation, about which you and I differ.

"In this connection let me ask your attention to another thing. I believe it is safe to assert that, five years ago, no living man had expressed the opinion that the Negro had no share in the Declaration of Independence.

"Let me state that again: Five years ago no living man had expressed the opinion that the Negro had no share in the Declaration of Independence. If there is in this large audience any man who ever knew of that opinion being put upon paper as much as five years ago, I will be obliged to him now, or at a subsequent time, to show it.

"If that be true, I wish you then to note the next fact—that within the space of five years Senator Douglas, in the argument of this question, has got his entire party, so far as I know, without exception, to join in saying that the Negro has no share in the Declaration of Independence. If there be now in all these United States one Douglas man that does not say this, I have been unable upon any occasion to scare him up. (Note by the writer: that expression "scare him up" makes me wish I could grab Abe around the neck and give him a hug, for it is an expression I have not heard for the twenty years I have lived in the city, and it brings back memories of scaring up rabbits in the fields.)

"Now, if none of you said this five years ago, and all of you say it now, that is a matter that you Kentuckians ought to note. That is a vast change in the Northern public sentiment upon that question.

"Of what tendency is that change? The tendency of that change is to bring the public mind to the conclusion that when men are spoken of, the Negro is not meant; that when Negroes are spoken of, brutes alone are contemplated. That change in public sentiment has already degraded the black man, in the estimation of Douglas and his followers, from the condition of a man of some sort, and assigned him to the condition of a brute. Now you Kentuckians ought to give Douglas credit for this. That is the largest possible stride that can be made in regard to the perpetuation of your good thing in slavery."

End of second quote.

Now, in order to show the reader where we started at, and how we have got to where we are now in regard to the Negro, I am going to quote the speech made by Senator Douglas at Jonesboro, Illinois, Sept. 15, 1858. It is the speech referred to by Mr. Lincoln in the above quote.

The reader will sense that the Negro got his first foothold among us because of the greed of politicians for votes. While the battle for offices raged, the Negro was fastening his hold on our country. Believe it or not, it is really a question now whether we are going to hold our own country, or is the Negro going to win out while we are not looking and take over. In the following speech Senator Douglas voices the sentiments of millions of real honest Americans.

MR. DOUGLAS'S STATEMENTS

Ladies and Gentlemen: I appear before you today in pursuance of a previous notice, and have made arrangements with Mr. Lincoln to divide time, and discuss with him the leading political topics that now agitate the country.

Prior to 1854 this country was divided into two great political parties known as Whig and Democratic. These parties differed from each other on certain questions which were then deemed to be important to the best interests of the republic. Whigs and Democrats differed about a bank, the tariff, distribution, the specie circular, and the subtreasury. On those issues we went before the country, and discussed the principles, objects, and measures of the two great parties. Each of the parties could proclaim its principles in Louisiana as well as in Massachusetts, in Kentucky as well as in Illinois. Since that period, a great revolution has taken place in the formation of parties, by which they now seem to be divided by a geographical line, a large party in the North being arrayed under the Abolition or Republican banner, in hostility to the Southern States, Southern people, and Southern institutions. It becomes important for us to inquire how this transformation of parties has occurred, made from those of national principles to geographical factions. You remember that in 1850—this country was agitated from its center to its circumference about this slavery question—it became necessary for the leaders of the great Whig party and the leaders of the great Democratic party to postpone for the time being their particular disputes, and unite first to save the Union before they should quarrel as to the mode in which it was to be governed. During the Congress of 1849-50, Henry Clay was the leader of the Union men, supported by Cass and Webster, and the leaders of the Democracy and the leaders of the Whigs, in opposition to Northern Abolitionists or Southern Disunionists. The great contest of 1850 resulted in the establishment of the compromise measures of that year, which measures rested on the great principle that the people of each State and each Territory of this Union ought to be permitted to regulate their own domestic institutions in their own way, subject to no other limitation than that which the Federal Constitution imposes.

I now wish to ask you whether that principle was right or wrong which guaranteed to every State and every community the right to form and regulate their domestic institutions to suit themselves. These measures were adopted, as I have previously said, by the joint action of the Union Whigs and Union Democrats in opposition to Northern Abolitionists and Southern Disunionists. In 1858, when the Whig party assembled at Baltimore in national convention for the last time, they adopted the principle of the compromise measures of 1850 as their rule of party action in the future. One month thereafter the Democrats assembled at the same place to nominate a candidate for the presidency, and declared the same great principle as the rule of action by which the Democracy would be governed.

The presidential election of 1852 was fought on that basis. It is true that the Whigs claimed special merit for the adoption of those measures, because they asserted that their great Clay originated them, their godlike Webster defended them, and their Fillmore signed the bill making them the law of the land; but on the other hand, the Democrats claimed special credit for the Democracy upon the ground that we gave twice as many votes in both houses of Congress for the passage of these measures as the Whig party.

Thus you see that in the presidential election of 1852 the Whigs were pledged by their platform and their candidate to the principle of the compromise measures of 1850, and the Democracy were likewise pledged by our principles, our platform, and our candidate to the same line of policy, to preserve peace and quiet between the different sections of this Union. Since that period the Whig party has been transformed into a sectional party, under the name of the Republican party, whilst the Democratic party continues the same national party it was at that day. All sectional men, all men of Abolition sentiments and principles, no matter whether they were old Abolitionists or had been Whigs or Democrats, rally under the sectional Republican banner, and consequently all national men, all Union-loving men, whether Whigs, Democrats, or by whatever name they have been known, ought to rally under the Stars and Stripes in defense of the Constitution as our fathers made it, and of the Union as it has existed under the Constitution.

How has this departure from the faith of the Democracy and the faith of the Whig party been accomplished? In 1854, certain restless, ambitious, and disappointed politicians throughout the land took advantage of the temporary excitement created by the Nebraska bill to try and dissolve the Old Whig party and the old Democratic party, to Abolitionize their members, and lead them, bound hand and foot, captives into the Abolition camp. In the State of New York a convention was held by some of these men, and a platform adopted, every plank of which was as black as night, each one relating to the Negro, and not one referring to the interests of the white man.

(Writer's note: As the reader knows, the Negro won out in this contest, for Lincoln was elected; and the Negro has been winning almost constantly ever since. Why is this? Do we white people hate one another so much that we would see ourselves dissolved into mulattoes before we will get together and do something about it)

That example was followed throughout the Northern States, the effort being made to combine all the free States in hostile array against the slave States. The men who thus thought that they could build up a great sectional party, and through its organization control the political destinies of this country, based all their hopes on the single fact that the North was the stronger division of the nation, and hence, if the North could be combined against the South, a sure victory awaited their efforts. I am doing no more than justice to the truth of history when I say that in this State Abraham Lincoln, on behalf of the Whigs, and Lyman Trumbull, on behalf of the Democrats, were the leaders who undertook to perform this grand scheme of Abolitionizing the two parties to which they belonged. They had a private arrangement as to what should be the political destiny of each of the contracting parties before they went into the operation. The arrangement was that Mr. Lincoln was to take the old-line Whigs with him, claiming that he was still as good a Whig as ever, over to the Abolitionists, and Mr. Trumbull was to run for Congress in the Belleville district, and, claiming to be a good Democrat, coax the old Democrats into the Abolition camp, and when, by the joint efforts of the Abolitionized Whigs, the Abolitionized Democrats, and the old-line Abolition and Free-soil party of this State, they should secure a majority in the legislature, Lincoln was then to be made United States senator in Shields' place, Trumbull remaining in Congress until I should be accommodating enough to die or resign, and give him a chance to follow Lincoln. That was a very nice little bargain so far as Lincoln and Trumbull were concerned, if it had been carried out in good faith, and friend Lincoln had attained to senatorial dignity according to the contract.

They went into the contest in every part of the State, calling upon all disappointed politicians to join in the crusade against the Democracy, and appealed to the prevailing sentiments and prejudices in all the northern counties of the State. In three congressional districts in the north end of the State they adopted, as the platform of this new party thus formed by Lincoln and Trumbull in connection with the Abolitionists, all of those principles which aimed at a warfare on the part of the North against the South. (Writer's note: He was right, all right, for the war came sure enough three years later.)

They declared in that platform that the Wilmot proviso was to be applied to all the Territories of the United States, North as well as South, and not only to all the territory we then had, but all that we might hereafter acquire; that hereafter no more slave States should be admitted into this Union, even if the people of such States desired slavery; that the fugitive-slave law should be absolutely and unconditionally repealed; that slavery should be abolished in the District of Columbia; that the slave-trade should be abolished between the different States, and, in fact, every article in their creed related to this slavery question, and pointed to a Northern geographical party in hostility to the Southern States of this Union.

Such were their principles in northern Illinois. A little further south they became bleached and grew paler just in proportion as public sentiment moderated and changed in this direction. There were Republicans or Abolitionists in the North, anti-Nebraska men down about Springfield, and in this neighborhood they contented themselves with talking about the inexpediency of the repeal of the Missouri Compromise. In the extreme northern counties they brought out men to canvass the State whose complexion suited their political creed, and hence Fred Douglas, the Negro, was to be found there, following General Cass, and attempting to speak on behalf of Lincoln, Trumbull, and Abolitionism, against that illustrious senator. Why, they brought Fred Douglas to Freeport, when I was addressing a meeting there, in a carriage driven by the white owner, the Negro sitting inside with the white lady and her daughter!

(Writer's note: We still have foolish and vain white women among us who would sell the white race down the river, but boy-o-boy, we'll know what to do with such when the time comes!)

When I got through canvassing the northern counties that year, and progressed as far south as Springfield, I was met and opposed in discussion by Lincoln, Lovejoy, Trumbull, and Sidney Breese, who were on one side. Father Giddings, the high priest of Abolitionism, had just been there, and Chase came about the time I left. (Voice: "Why didn't you shoot him?")

I did take a running shot at them, but as I was singlehanded against the white, black, and mixed drove, I had to use a shot-gun and fire into the crowd instead of taking them off singly with a rifle.

Trumbull had for his lieutenants in aiding him to Abolitionize the Democracy, such men as John Wentworth of Chicago, Governor Reynolds of Belleville, Sidney Breese of Carlisle, and John Dougherty of Union, each of whom modified his opinions to suit the locality he was in. Dougherty, for instance, would not go much further than to talk about the inexpediency of the Nebraska bill, whilst his allies at Chicago advocated Negro citizenship and Negro equality, putting the white man and the Negro on the same basis under the law. Now these men, four years ago, were engaged in a conspiracy to break down the Democracy; today they are again acting together for the same purpose!

They do not hoist the same flag; they do not own the same principles, or profess the same faith; but to conceal their union for the sake of policy. In the northern counties you find that all the conventions are called in the name of the Black Republican party; at Springfield they dare not call a Republican convention, but invite all the enemies of the Democracy to unite, and when they get down into Egypt, Trumbull issues notices calling upon the "Free Democracy" to assemble and hear him speak.

I have one of the handbills calling a Trumbull meeting at Waterloo the other day, which I received there, which is in the following language: "A meeting of the Free Democracy will take place in Waterloo, on Monday, Sept. 13th inst., whereat Hon. Lyman Trumbull, Hon. Jehu Baker, and others will address the people upon the different political topics of the day. Members of all parties are cordially invited to be present and hear and determine for themselves."

—*The Monroe Free Democracy*

What is that name of "Free Democrats" put forth for unless to deceive the people, and make them believe that Trumbull and his followers are not the same party as that which raises the black flag of

Abolitionism in the northern part of the State, and makes war upon the Democratic party throughout the State? When I put that question to them at Waterloo on Saturday last, one of them rose and stated that they had changed their name for political effect in order to get votes. There was a candid admission.

Their object in changing their party organization and principles in different localities was avowed to be an attempt to cheat and deceive some portion of the people until after the election. Why cannot a political party that is conscious of the rectitude of its purposes and the soundness of its principles declare them everywhere alike? I would disdain to hold any political principles that I could not avow in the same terms in Kentucky that I declared in Illinois, in Charleston as well as in Chicago, in New Orleans as well as in New York. So long as we live under a Constitution common to all the States, our political faith ought to be as broad, as liberal, and just as that Constitution itself, and should be proclaimed alike in every portion of the Union. But it is apparent that our opponents find it necessary, for the partizan effect, to change their colors in different counties in order to catch the popular breeze, and hope with these discordant materials combined together to secure a majority in the legislature for the purpose of putting down the Democratic party. This combination did succeed in 1854 so far as to elect a majority of their confederates to the legislature, and the first important act which they performed was to elect a senator in the place of the eminent and gallant Senator Shields. He had served the people of the State with ability in the legislature, he had served you with fidelity and ability as auditor, he had performed his duties to the satisfaction of the whole country at the head of the Land Department at Washington, he had covered the State and the Union with immortal glory on the bloody fields of Mexico in defense of the honor of the flag, and yet he had to be stricken down by this unholy combination. And for what cause? Merely because he would not join in a combination of one-half of the States to make war upon the other half, after having poured out his heart's blood for all the States of the Union. Trumbull was put in his place by Abolitionism.

How did Trumbull get there?

Before the Abolitionists would consent to go into an election for United States senator, they required all members of this new combination to show their hands upon this question of Abolitionism. Lovejoy, one of the high priests, brought in resolutions defining the Abolition creed, and required them to commit themselves on it by their votes—yea or nay. In that creed as laid down by Lovejoy, they declared first, that the Wilmot proviso must be put on all the Territories of the United States, north and south, and that no more territory should ever be acquired unless slavery was first prohibited therein; second, that no more States should ever be received into the Union unless slavery was first prohibited, by constitutional provision, in such States; third, that the fugitive-slave law must be immediately repealed, or, failing in that, then such amendments were to be made to it as would render it useless and inefficient for the objects for which it was passed, etc. The next day after these resolutions were offered they were voted upon, part of them carried, and the others defeated, the same men who voted for them, with only two exceptions, voting soon after for Abraham Lincoln as their candidate for the United States Senate.

He came within one or two votes of being elected, but he could not quite get the number required, for the simple reason that his friend Trumbull, who was a party to the bargain by which Lincoln was to take Shields' place, controlled a few Abolitionized Democrats in the legislature, and would not allow them all to vote for him, thus wronging Lincoln by permitting him on each ballot to be almost elected, but not quite, until he forced them to drop Lincoln and elect him (Trumbull), in order to unite the party. Thus you find that although the legislature was carried that year by the bargain between Trumbull, Lincoln, and the Abolitionists, and the union of these discordant elements in one harmonious party, yet Trumbull violated his pledge, and played a Yankee trick on Lincoln when they came to divide the spoils.

Perhaps you would like a little evidence on this point. If you would, I will call Colonel James H. Matheny of Springfield, to the stand, Mr. Lincoln's especial confidential friend for the last twenty years, and see what he will say upon the subject of this bargain. Matheny is now the Black Republican or Abolition candidate for Congress in the Springfield district against the gallant Colonel Harris, and is making speeches all over that part of the State against me and in favor of Lincoln, in concert with Trumbull. He ought to be a good witness, and I will read an extract from a speech which he made in 1856, when he was mad because his friend Lincoln had been cheated.

It is one of the numerous speeches of the same tenor that were made about that time, exposing this bargain between Lincoln, Trumbull, and the Abolitionists. Matheny said: (reading)

> The Whigs, Abolitonists, Know-nothings, and renegade Democrats made a solemn compact for the purpose of carrying this State against the Democracy, on this plan: First, that they would all combine and elect Mr. Trumbull to Congress, and thereby carry his district for the legislature, in order to throw all the strength that could be obtained into that body against the Democrats; second, that when the legislature should meet, the officers of that body, such as speaker, clerks, doorkeepers, etc., would be given to the Abolitionists; and third, that the Whigs were

to have the United States senator. That, accordingly, in good faith, Trumbull was elected to Congress, and his district carried for the legislature, and, when it convened, the Abolitionists got all the officers of that body, and thus far the "bond" was fairly executed. The Whigs, on their part, demanded the election of Abraham Lincoln to the United States Senate, that the bond might be fulfilled, the other parties to the contract having already secured to themselves all that was called for.

But, in the most perfidious manner, they refused to elect Mr. Lincoln; and the mean, low-lived, sneaking Trumbull succeeded, by pledging all that was required by any party, in thrusting Lincoln aside and foisting himself, an excrescence from the rotten bowels of the Democracy, into the United States Senate; and thus it has ever been, that an honest man makes a bad bargain when he conspires or contracts with rogues.

Matheny thought that his friend Lincoln made a bad bargain when he conspired and contracted with such rogues as Trumbull and his Abolition associates in that campaign. Lincoln was shoved off the track, and he and his friends all at once began to mope; became sour and mad, and disposed to tell, but dare not; and thus they stood for a long time, until the Abolitionists coaxed and flattered him back by their assurances that he should certainly be a senator in my place. In that way the Abolitionists have been able to hold Lincoln to the alliance up to this time, and now they have brought him into a fight against me, and he is to see if he is again to be cheated by them. Lincoln this time, though, required more of them than a promise, and holds their bond, if not security, that Lovejoy shall not cheat him as Trumbull did.

When the Republican convention assembled at Springfield in June last, for the purpose of nominating State officers only, the Abolitionists could not get Lincoln and his friends into it until they would pledge themselves that Lincoln should be their candidate for the Senate; and you will find, in proof of this, that that convention passed a resolution, unanimously declaring that Abraham Lincoln was the "first, last, and only choice" of the Republicans for United States senator. He was not willing to have it understood that he was merely their first choice, or their last choice, but their only choice. The Black Republican party had nobody else. Browning was nowhere; Governor Bissell was of no account; Archie Williams was not to be taken into consideration; John Wentworth was not worth mentioning; John M. Palmer was degraded; and their party presented the extraordinary spectacle of having but one—the first, the last, and only choice for the Senate. Suppose that Mr. Lincoln should die, what a horrible condition the Republican party would be in! They would have nobody left. They have no other choice, and it was necessary for them to put themselves before the world in this ludicrous, ridiculous attitude of having no other choice in order to quiet Lincoln's suspicions, and assure him that he was not to be cheated by Lovejoy, and the trickery by which Trumbull out-generaled him. Well, gentlemen, I think they will have a nice time of it before they get through. I do not intend to give them any chance to cheat Lincoln at all this time. I intend to relieve him of all anxiety upon that subject, and spare them the mortification of more exposures of contracts violated, and the pledged honor of rogues forfeited.

But I wish to invite your attention to the chief points at issue between Mr. Lincoln and myself in this discussion. Mr. Lincoln, knowing that he was to be the candidate of his party on account of the arrangement of which I have already spoken, knowing that he was to receive the nomination of the convention for the United States

Senate, had his speech, accepting that nomination, all written and committed to memory, ready to be delivered the moment the nomination was announced. Accordingly, when it was made he was in readiness and delivered his speech, a portion of which I will read in order that I may state his political principles fairly, by repeating them in his own language: (reading)

> We are now far into the fifth year since a policy was instituted for the avowed object, and with the confident promise of putting an end to slavery agitation; under the operation of that policy, that agitation has not only not ceased, but has constantly augmented. I believe it will not cease until a crisis shall have been reached and passed. "A house divided against itself cannot stand." I believe this government cannot endure permanently half slave and half free. I do not expect the Union to be dissolved— I do not expect the house to fall—but I do expect that it will cease to be divided.
>
> It will become all one thing or all the other. Either the opponents of slavery will arrest the spread of it, and place it where the public mind shall rest in the belief that it is in the course of ultimate extinction, or its advocates will push it forward until it shall become alike lawful in all the States, North as well as South.

There you have Mr. Lincoln's first and main proposition, upon which he bases his claims, stated in his own language. He tells you that this republic cannot endure permanently divided into slave and free States, as our fathers made it. He says that they must all become free or all become slave, that they must all be one thing or all be the other, or this government cannot last. Why can it not last, if we will execute the government in the same spirit and upon the same principles upon which it was founded?

Lincoln, by his proposition, says to the South, "If you desire to maintain your institutions as they are now, you must not be satisfied with minding your own business, but you must invade Illinois and all the other Northern States, establish slavery in them, and make it universal"; and in the same language he says to the North, "You must not be content with regulating your own affairs, and minding your own business, but if you desire to maintain your freedom, you must invade the Southern States, abolish slavery there and everywhere, in order to have the States all one thing or all the other." I say that this is the inevitable and irresistible result of Mr. Lincoln's argument, inviting a warfare between the North and the South, to be carried on with ruthless vengeance, until the one section or the other shall be driven to the wall, and become the victim of the rapacity of the other. (Writer's note: Boy! he saw what was coming, didn't he!)

What good would follow such a system of warfare? Suppose the North should succeed in conquering the South, how much would she be the gainer? Or suppose the South should conquer the North, could the Union be preserved in that way? Is this sectional warfare to be waged between Northern States and Southern States until they shall become uniform in their local and domestic institutions, merely because Mr. Lincoln says that a house divided against itself cannot stand, and pretends that this scriptural quotation, this language of our Lord and Master, is applicable to the American Union and the American Constitution? Washington and his compeers, in the convention that framed the Constitution, made this government divided into free and slave States. It was composed then of thirteen sovereign and independent States, each having sovereign authority over its local and domestic institutions, and all bound together by the Federal Constitution.

Mr. Lincoln likens that bond of the Federal Constitution, joining free and slave States together, to a house divided against itself, and says that it is contrary to the law of God and cannot stand. It has stood thus divided into free and slave States from its organization up to this day.

During that period we have increased from four millions to thirty millions of people; we have extended our territory from the Mississippi to the Pacific ocean; we have acquired the Floridas and Texas, and other territory sufficient to double our geographical extent; we have increased in population, in wealth, and in power beyond any example on Earth; we have risen from a weak and feeble power to become the terror and admiration of the civilized world; and all this has been done under a Constitution which Mr. Lincoln, in substance, says is in violation of the law of God, and under a Union divided into free and slave States, which Mr. Lincoln thinks, because of such division, cannot stand. Surely Mr. Lincoln is a wiser man than those who framed the government. Washington did not believe, nor did his compatriots, that the local laws and domestic institutions that were adapted to the Green Mountains of Vermont were suited to the rice plantations of South Carolina; they did not believe at that day that in a republic so broad and expanded as this, containing such a variety of climate, soil, and interest, uniformity in the local laws and domestic institutions was either desirable or possible. They believed then, as our experience has proved to us now, that each locality, having different interests, a different climate, and different surroundings, required different local laws, local policy, and local institutions, adapted to the wants of that locality. Thus our government was formed on the principle of diversity in the local institutions and laws, and not on that of uniformity.

As my time flies, I can only glance at these points and not present them as fully as I would wish, because I desire to bring all the points

CHAPTER ONE | 51

in controversy between the two parties before you in order to have Mr. Lincoln's reply. He makes war on the decision of the Supreme Court, in the case known as the Dred Scott case. I wish to say to you, fellow-citizens, that I have no war to make on that decision, or any other rendered by the Supreme Court. I am content to take that decision as it stands delivered by the highest tribunal on Earth, a judicial tribunal established by the Constitution of the United States for that purpose, and hence that decision becomes the law of the land, binding on you, on me, and on every other good citizen, whether we like it or not. Hence I do not choose to go into an argument to prove, before this audience, whether or not Chief Justice Taney understood the law better than Abraham Lincoln.

Mr. Lincoln objects to that decision, first and mainly because it deprives the Negro of the rights of citizenship. I am as much opposed to his reason for the objection as I am to the objection itself. I hold that a Negro is not and never ought to be a citizen of the United States. I hold that this government was made on the white basis, by white men for the benefit of white men and their posterity forever, and should be administered by white men, and none others. I do not believe that the Almighty made the Negro capable of self-government. I am aware that all the Abolition lecturers that you find traveling about through the country, are in the habit of reading the Declaration of Independence to prove that all men were created equal and endowed by the Creator with certain inalienable rights, among which are life, liberty, and the pursuit of happiness. Mr. Lincoln is very much in the habit of following in the track of Lovejoy in this particular, by reading that part of the Declaration of Independence to prove that the Negro was endowed by the Almighty with the inalienable right of equality with white men.

(Writer's note: Isn't it strange, dear reader, that a man with the brains of the illustrious Douglas did not think of or finish that reasoning? Well, here it is: If the Almighty gave the black man the inalienable right to social equality with the white man, then He gave the black man the right to destroy the white man, for that is exactly what would happen by the indiscriminate mixing up of the two races. Would any man in his right mind stand up and try to tell me that this would not happen? Any man who would contend that the two races can mix socially without the eventual disappearance of the white race is either a fool or crazy, or both.)

Now, I say to you, my fellow-citizens, that in my opinion the signers of the Declaration had no reference to the Negro whatever, when they declared all men to be created equal. They desired to express by that phrase white men, men of European birth and European descent, and had no reference either to the Negro, the savage Indians, the Feegee, the Malay, or any other inferior and degraded race, when they spoke of the equality of men. One great evidence that such was their understanding, is to be found in the fact that at that time every one of the thirteen colonies was a slaveholding colony, every signer of the Declaration represented a slaveholding constituency, and we know that no one of them emancipated his slaves, much less offered citizenship to them, when they signed the Declaration; and yet, if they intended to declare that the Negro was the equal of the white man, and entitled by divine right to an equality with him, they were bound, as honest men, that day and hour to have put their Negroes on an equality with themselves. Instead of doing so, with uplifted eyes to heaven they implored the divine blessing upon them, during the seven years' bloody war they had to fight to maintain that Declaration, never dreaming that they were violating divine law by still holding the Negroes in bondage and depriving them of equality.

My friends, I am in favor of preserving this government as our fathers made it. It does not follow by any means that because the Negro is not your equal or mine, that hence he must necessarily be a slave. On the contrary, it does follow that we ought to extend to the Negro every right, every privilege, every immunity which he is capable of enjoying, consistent with the safety of our society. When you ask me what these rights are, what their nature and extent is, I tell you that that is a question which each State of this Union must decide for itself. Illinois has already decided the question. We have decided that the Negro must not be a slave within our limits; but we have also decided that the Negro shall not be a citizen within our limits; that he shall not vote, hold office, or exercise any political rights. I maintain that Illinois, as a sovereign State, has a right thus to fix her policy with reference to the relation between the white man and the Negro; but while we had that right to decide the question for ourselves, we must recognize the same right for Kentucky and for every other State to make the same decision, or a different one. Having decided our own policy with reference to the black race, we must leave Kentucky and Missouri and every other State perfectly free to make just such a decision as they see proper on that question.

(Writer's note: Had this policy been adhered to there could have been no Civil War, and we would not have that blot on our history. Still, if Harriet Beecher Stowe had died in her cradle, and that lying Uncle Tom's Cabin had never been written, maybe the war could have been avoided. If you don't believe that that book was full of lies, just read up on other literature of that period and see how surprised the people of the North were to find that the slaves would neither desert, nor take up arms against their former masters. The truth is that the slaves took up arms to protect their "white folks" from them damn interferin' Northerners.)

Kentucky has decided that question for herself. She has said that within her limits a Negro shall not exercise any political rights, and she has also said that a portion of the Negroes under the laws of that State shall be slaves. She had as much right to adopt that as her policy as we had to adopt the contrary for our policy. New York has decided that in that State a Negro may vote if he has two hundred and fifty dollars' worth of property, and if he owns that much he may vote upon an equality with the white man.

(Writer's note: And do you, reader, see how that policy would work today. Why, all the Negroes could vote. You know how they would do it? The National Association for the Advancement of Colored People would be right down there at the polls, and the same two hundred and fifty dollars would be used over and over again, as fast as they could get into line.)

I, for one, (Writer's note: Me too!) am utterly opposed to Negro suffrage anywhere and under any circumstances; (Writer's note: Why am I opposed to Negro suffrage? I'll tell you why—because giving the Negro the right to vote in a white country is tantamount to giving him the right to utterly destroy the white race. Just you, reader, watch New York with its Communists and Negroes on the city council. They'll be forcing white people to take a certain proportion of Negroes to their afternoon teas next. Just you wait and see. Yet, inasmuch as the Supreme Court has decided in the celebrated Dred Scott case that a State has the right to confer the privilege of voting upon free Negroes, I am not going to make war upon New York because she has adopted a policy repugnant to my feelings. But New York must mind her own business, and keep her Negro suffrage to herself, and not attempt to force it upon us.

In the State of Maine they have decided that a Negro may vote and hold office on an equality with a white man. (Writer's note: Could it be possible that the people of Maine were so thick skulled that they could not see the danger to the white race from such a policy?

Would they maintain that a mulatto, with her yellow death-like skin, and awful hair, is as beautiful as our lovely blue-eyed blondes with their Dresden china skin? Such people—tch, tch.) I had occasion to say to the senators from Maine, in a discussion last session, that if they thought that the white people within the limits of their State were no better than Negroes, I would not quarrel with them for it, but they must not say that my white constituents of Illinois were no better than Negroes, or we would be sure to quarrel.

(Writer's note: Hooray for Douglas! There's a man for you. Come on now and give him three cheers—h-ray, h-ray, h-ray!!)

The Dred Scott decision covers the whole question, and declares that each State has the right to settle this question of suffrage for itself, and all questions as to the relations between the white man and the Negro.

Judge Taney expressly lays down the doctrine. I receive it as law, and I say that while those States are adopting regulations on that subject disgusting and abhorrent, according to my views, I will not make war on them if they will mind their own business and let us alone.

(Writer's note: Now, reader, I want to ask you a question. Do you think that it is possible that our brain develops further with each generation, and what was an instinct in an earlier generation comes to the surface in a later generation, and the later generation can put the instinct into words? Take this business of fighting off the black race—our early ancestors must have fought the black race with all the ferociousness of wounded tigers, for if they had not, there would surely be no white people left at this late day, and yet it was only natural instinct which made them fight, for as we have read above, even the people of Maine did not yet realize consciously that giving the vote to the black race might lead to the end of the white, or surely they would not have conferred that right on them.)

I now come back to the question, why cannot this Union exist forever divided into free and slave States, as our fathers made it? (Writer's note: It seems rather peculiar that Judge Douglas could not see that slavery would gradually die out, as knowledge and education advanced.) It can thus exist if each State will carry out the principles upon which our institutions were founded—to wit, the right of each State to do as it pleases, without meddling with its neighbors. Just act upon that great principle, and this Union will not only live forever, but it will extend and expand until it covers the whole continent, and makes this confederacy one grand, ocean-bound republic. We must bear in mind that we are yet a young nation, growing with a rapidity unequaled in the history of the world, that our national increase is great, and that the emigration from the Old World is increasing, requiring us to expand and acquire new territory from time to time in order to give our people land to live upon.

If we live up to the principle of State rights and State sovereignty, each State regulating its own affairs and minding its own business, we can go on and extend indefinitely, just as fast and far as we need the territory.

The time may come, indeed has now come, when our interests would be advanced by the acquisition of the island of Cuba. When we get Cuba we must take it as we find it, leaving the people to decide the question of slavery for themselves, without interference on the part of the Federal Government, or of any State of the Union. So when it becomes necessary to acquire any portion of Mexico or Canada, or of this continent or the adjoining islands, we must take them as we find them, leaving the people free to do as they please—to have slavery or not, as they choose. I never have inquired, and never will inquire, whether a new State applying for admission has slavery or not for one of her institutions. If the constitution that is presented be the act and deed of the people, and embodies their will, and they have the requisite population, I will admit them with slavery or without it, just as that people shall determine. My objection to the Lecompton constitution did not consist in the fact that it made Kansas a slave State. I would have been as much opposed to its admission under such a constitution as a free State as I was opposed to its admission under it as a slave State. I hold that that was a question which that people had a right to decide for themselves, and that no power on Earth ought to have interfered with that decision. In my opinion, the Lecompton constitution was not the act and deed of the people of Kansas, and did not embody their will, and the recent election in that Territory, at which it was voted down by nearly ten to one, shows conclusively that I was right in saying, when the constitution was presented, that it was not the act and deed of the people, and did not embody their will. If we wish to preserve our institutions in their purity, and transmit them unimpaired to our latest posterity, we must preserve with religious good faith that great principle of self-government which guarantees to each and every State, old and new, the right to make just such constitutions as they desire, and come into the Union with their own constitution, and not one palmed upon them.

Whenever you sanction the doctrine that Congress may crowd a constitution down the throats of an unwilling people, against their consent, you will subvert the great fundamental principle upon which all our free institutions rest. In the future I have no fear that the attempt will ever be made. (Writer's note: Wouldn't Mr. Douglas just love to be here and know what the New Deal has been trying to do for ten years?)

President Buchanan declared in his annual message, that hereafter the rule adopted in the Minnesota case, requiring a constitution to be submitted to the people, should be followed in all future cases, and if he stands by that recommendation there will be no division in the Democratic party on that principle in the future. Hence the great mission of the Democracy is to unite the fraternal feeling of the whole country, restore peace and quiet by teaching each State to mind its own business and regulate its own domestic affairs, (Writer's note: Let that radical crowd in New York State take heed and calm down about the poll tax in the Southern States!) and all unite in carrying out the Constitution as our fathers made it, and thus to preserve the Union and render it perpetual in all time to come. Why should we not act as our fathers who made the government? There was no sectional strife in Washington's army. They were all brethren of a common confederacy; they fought under a common flag that they might bestow upon their posterity a common destiny, and to this end they poured out their blood in common streams, and shared, in some instances, a common grave." (Writer's note: Amen!)

End of third quote.

President Abraham Lincoln was a strict segregationist, and a believer in the necessity of white supremacy, as far as the black and white races were concerned; a fact that not many people living today know. In a speech made at Springfield, Illinois, on June 26, 1857— he said:

> There is a natural disgust in the minds of nearly all white people at the idea of an indiscriminate amalgamation of the white and black races . . . A separation of the races is the only perfect preventive of amalgamation; but as an immediate separation is impossible the next best thing is to keep them apart where they are not already together. If white and black people never get together in Kansas, they will never mix blood in Kansas. This is at least one self-evident truth. A few free colored persons may get into the free States, in any event; but their number is too insignificant to amount to much in the way of

mixing blood . . .

Such separation, if it ever be effected at all, must be effected by colonization; and no political party, as such, is now doing anything directly for colonization. Party operations at present only favor or retard colonization incidentally. The enterprise is a difficult one, but, "where there is a will there is a way," and what colonization needs most is a hearty will. Will springs from the two elements of moral sense and self-interest.

Let us be brought to believe it is morally right, and at the same time favorable to, or at least not against, our interest to transfer the African to his native clime, and we shall find a way to do it, however great the task may be. The children of Israel, to such numbers as to include four hundred thousand fighting men, went out of Egyptian bondage in a body.

The reader can thus understand what a tragedy it really was for the great Lincoln to be snuffed out by an assassin's bullet just when the Country needed him most. He was determined to put the South back in good order immediately after hostilities ceased. But John Wilkes Booth laid low this great and good man, and placed the South under the heels of mean and vicious men. If you read Lincoln's life you will see that he would not stand for atrocities, and always demanded immediate and full reports on all those reported. Had he lived Negro troops would never have been sent into the South during the terrible days of reconstruction, and it is more than probable that we would not have the Negro problem, at this late day, which he wished to settle, now towering over us like a monstrous black dragon, threatening to completely annihilate us.

Here's what Robert E. Lee said in regard to this Negro problem:

> The only reason why I have allowed myself to own a slave for a moment is the insoluble problem of what to do with him when freed. The one excuse for slavery which the South can plead without fear before the Judgement bar of God is the blacker problem which their emancipation will create. We've played our parts, gentlemen, in a hopeless tragedy, pitiful, terrible. At least eight thousand of our sons are dead or mangled. A million more will die of poverty and disease. Every issue could have been settled and better settled without the loss of a drop of blood. The slaves are freed by an accident. An accident of war's necessity—not on principle. The manner of their sudden emancipation, unless they are removed, will bring a calamity more apalling than the war itself. It must create a race problem destined to grow each day more threatening and insoluble . . .

And this is what Robert Toombs (Senator) said:

> The question before you is bigger than the South. It is bigger than the Republic. It is bigger than the Continent. It may involve the future of civilization.
>
> The employment of these Negro troops, clothed in the uniform of the Union, marks the lowest tide mud to which its citizenship has ever sunk. The profoundest word in history is Race. The ancestral soul of a people rules its destiny.
>
> What is the ancestral soul of the Negro? Has the Negro moved upward? This Republic was born of the soul of a race of pioneer white freemen who settled on our continent and built an altar within its forest cathedral to Lib-

erty and Progress. In the record of man has the Negro ever dreamed this dream?

The Roman Republic fell and Rome became a degenerate Empire. Why? Because of the lowering of her racial stock by slaves. The decline of the Roman spirit was due to a mixture of races. The flower of her manhood died on her far-flung battle lines. Slaves and degenerates at home bred her future citizens.

Have we also placed our feet on the path to oblivion? History is littered with the wrecks of civilizations. And always the secret is found in racial degeneracy—the lowering of the standard of racial values.

Civilization is a name—an effect. Race is the cause. If a race maintains its soul, it must remain itself and it must breed its best. Race is the result of thousands of years of this selection. One drop of Negro blood makes a Negro. The inferior always blot out the superior if granted social equality.

Putting this soldier's uniform on the Negro is the first step toward racial oblivion for the white man in America. It is the first step toward equality. A half-breed people have no soul. They are always ungovernable. The Negro is the lowest species of man . . .

In the meantime we hold fast to the faith within us. Dare to arm the Negro, drill and teach him to kill white men, and we become traitors to our country, traitors to humanity, and traitors to civilization. Robert E. Lee is himself the supreme contradiction to the suicidal mush involved in the dogma of equality. His genius and character are racial products . . .

Now this one last quotation from an address by Abraham Lincoln, made to a Deputation of Colored Men on August 14, 1862, at Washington, on the subject of Colonization.

They were all seated, and the President began:

"You and we are different races. We have between us a broader difference than exists between almost any other two races. Whether it be right or wrong I need not discuss; but this physical difference is a great disadvantage to us both, as I think. Your race suffer very greatly, many of them, by living among us, while ours suffer from your presence. In a word, we suffer on each side. If this is admitted, it affords a reason, at least, why we should be separated. You here are freemen, I suppose? (A voice: "Yes, Sir.")

"Perhaps you have long been free, or all your lives. Your race is suffering, in my judgment, the greatest wrong inflicted on any people. But even when you cease to be slaves, you are yet far removed from being placed on an equality with the white people. You are cut off from many of the advantages that the other race enjoys.

"The aspiration of men is to enjoy equality with the best when free, but on this broad continent not a single man of your race is made the equal of a single man of ours. Go where you are treated the best, and the ban is still upon you. I do not propose to discuss this, but to present it as a fact with which we have to deal. I cannot alter it if I would. It is a fact about which we all think and feel alike, I and you. We look to our condition.

"Owing to the existence of the two races on this continent, I need not recount to you the effects upon white men, growing out of the institution of slavery.

"I believe in its general evil effects upon the white race. See our present condition—the country engaged in war—our white men cutting one another's throats—none knowing how far it will extend—and then consider what we know to be the truth. But for your race among us there could be no war, although many men engaged on either side do not care for you one way or the other. Nevertheless, I repeat, without the institution of slavery, and the colored race the cause, the war could not have an existence. It is better for us both, therefore, to be separated.

"I know that there are free men among you who, even if they could better their condition, are not as much inclined to go out of the country as those who, being slaves, could obtain their freedom on this condition. I suppose one of the principal difficulties in the way of colonization is that the free colored man cannot see that his comfort would be advanced by it.

"You may believe that you can live in Washington, or elsewhere in the United States, the remainder of your life as easily, perhaps more so, than you can in any foreign country; and hence you may come to the conclusion that you have nothing to do with the idea of going to a foreign country.

"This is (I speak in no unkind sense) an extremely selfish view of the case. You ought to do something to help those who are not so fortunate as yourselves. There is an unwillingness on the part of our people, harsh as it may be, for you free colored people to remain with us. Now, if you could give a start to the white people, you would open a wide door for many to be made free. If we deal with those who are not free at the beginning, and whose intellects are clouded by slavery, we have very poor material to start with. If intelligent colored men, such as are before me, would move in this matter, much might be accomplished. It is exceedingly important that we have men at the beginning capable of thinking as white men, and not those who have been systematically oppressed. There is much to encourage you. For the sake of your race you should sacrifice something of your present comfort for the purpose of being as grand in that respect as the white people. It is a cheering thought throughout life, that something can be done to ameliorate the condition of those who have been subject to the hard usages of the world. It is difficult to make a man miserable while he feels he is worthy of himself and claims kindred to the great God who made him.

"In the American Revolutionary war sacrifices were made by men engaged in it, but they were cheered by the future. (Writer's note: Let's not forget that the great Thomas Paine was the man who pointed out the future to Washington's soldiers. Remember? "The sunshine patriot, and the summertime soldier, etc.")

"General Washington himself endured greater physical hardships than if he had remained a British subject, yet he was a happy man because he was engaged in benefiting his race, in doing something for the children of his neighbors, having none of his own.

"The colony of Liberia has been in existence for a long time. (Writer's note: This Negro republic was formed in 1847 to provide a native home for freed slaves from America.) In a certain sense it is a success.

"The old President of Liberia, Roberts, has just been with me—the first time I ever saw him. He says they have within the bounds of that colony between three and four hundred thousand people, or more than in some of our old States, such as Rhode Island or Delaware, or in some of our newer States, and less than in some of our larger ones. They are not all American Negro colonists or their descendants. Something less than 12,000 have been sent thither from this country. Many of the original settlers have died; yet, like people elsewhere, their offspring outnumber those deceased.

"The question is, if the colored people are persuaded to go anywhere, why not there?

"One reason for unwillingness to do so is that some of you would rather remain within reach of the country of your nativity. I do not know how much attachment you may have towards our race.

It does not strike me that you have the greatest reason to love them. But still you are attached to them, at all events.

"The place I am thinking about for a colony is in Central America. It is nearer to us than Liberia—not much more than one-fourth as far as Liberia, and within seven days' run by steamers. Unlike Liberia, it is a great line of travel—it is a highway. The country is a very excellent one for any people, and with great natural resources and advantages, and especially because of the similarity of climate with your native soil, thus being suited to your physical condition. The particular place I have in view is to be a great highway from the Atlantic or Caribbean Sea to the Pacific Ocean, and this particular place has all the advantages for a colony.

"On both sides there are harbors—among the finest in the world. Again, there is evidence of very rich coal mines. A certain amount of coal is valuable in any country. Why I attach so much importance to coal is, it will afford an opportunity to the inhabitants for immediate employment till they get ready to settle permanently in their homes. If you take colonists where there is no good landing, there is a bad show, and so where there is nothing to cultivate and of which to make a farm. But if something is started so that you can get your daily bread as soon as you reach there, it is a great advantage. Coal land is the best thing I know of with which to commence an enterprise.

"To return—you have been talked to upon this subject, and told that a speculation is intended by gentlemen who have an interest in that country, including the coal mines. We have been mistaken all our lives if we do not know whites, as well as blacks, look to their own self-interest.

"Unless among those of deficient intellect, everybody you trade with makes something. You meet with these things here and everywhere. If such persons have what will be an advantage to them, the question is, whether it cannot be made of advantage to you? You are intelligent, and know that success does not so much depend on external help as on self-reliance. Much, therefore, depends upon yourselves. As to the coal mines, I think I see the means available for your self-reliance. I shall, if I get a sufficient number of you engaged, have provision made that you shall not be wronged. If you will engage in the enterprise, I will spend some of the money intrusted to me. I am not sure you will succeed. The government may lose the money, but we cannot succeed unless we try; and we think, with care, we can succeed. The political affairs in Central America are not in quite as satisfactory condition as I wish. There are contending factions in that quarter; but, it is true, all factions are agreed alike on the subject of colonization, and want it, and are more generous than we are here.

"To your colored race they have no objection. I would endeavor to have you made the equals, and have the best assurance that you should be, the equals of the best.

"The practical thing I want to ascertain is, whether I can get a number of able-bodied men, with their wives and children, who are willing to go when I present evidence of encouragement and protection. Could I get a hundred tolerably intelligent men, with their wives and children, and able to "cut their own fodder," so to speak?

"Can I have fifty? If I could find twenty-five able-bodied men, with a mixture of women and children—good things in the family relation, I think—I could make a successful commencement. I want you to let me know whether this can be done or not. This is the practical part of my wish to see you. These are subjects of very great importance—worthy of a month's study, instead of a speech delivered in an hour. I ask you, then, to consider seriously, not pertaining to yourselves merely, nor for your race and ours of the present time, but as one of the things, if successfully managed, for the good of mankind—not confined to the present generation, but as: "From age to age descends the lay; To millions yet to be; Till far its echoes roll away; Into eternity."

End of quote.

When Wendell Willkie stated that hereafter this was going to be "one world" he almost hit it, but not quite, as there are going to be two worlds; one white and the other colored. With the fast means of transportation which we will develop after this war, a man's resident and native country is not going to mean quite as much as it has in the past. A white man's country will be any white country, and a colored man's country will be any colored country. When any white country is attacked by colored troops it will be the business of every white country to rush to its defense, and vice versa.

Now, to return to our present Negro problem. This problem has not been solved, and the public mind must now be focused upon it. Indeed, this problem, if not solved soon, will grow and grow until it can be settled only by more bloodshed. Obviously, a nation of men with the intelligence we credit ourselves with should look to the future, and not permit such a calamity to come to pass.

We, as a people, are prone to let matters just drift along, hoping that everything will come out all right. It is our nature not to face a thing until we are compelled to do so. Consider the malicious attack by the Japanese on Pearl Harbor. Our War Department knew that that attack was coming sooner or later, but nothing effective was done to meet it, with the sad result that hundreds of our boys lost their lives in a shameful manner, and our Navy was crippled. Why must we always wait until we have been slugged unmercifully before we fight back?

If that attack wakes us up to the fact that problems have a way of growing and growing until they come to a head, instead of solving themselves, it will have served a good and useful purpose.

The great problem which we now face, is not a new problem, but an old one which has been growing since the end of the Civil War. That problem, simply stated, is: *How can we do right by the Negro, and at the same time preserve the white race?* We are a sympathetic people. We do not believe in cruelty, even to animals. Therefore, we shall have to work out a solution which will be fair to the Negro, and at the same time maintain our integrity.

We cannot blame the Negro himself, if he cares little whether we maintain our integrity or not. His own welfare concerns him more than anything else, and if he has to pull the white race down in order to get on top, no one can say that he is inhuman to try to do it.

But we are in power now, and it is up to us to arrange our own country in such a way that, while the Negro will have a State of his own, where he can enjoy all of the things the world offers, and can have his own government, with opportunities for all, he will never be tempted to overthrow the white people. Our descendants are crying to us to do this, so that they will not have to come to unequal grips with them, and perhaps be wiped off the Earth.

No other nation on this Earth has this stupendous problem staring it in the face, and rapidly coming to a head. We have got to solve it, and solve it right, or we shall be despised and hated by our descendants, and we shall deserve it.

Being the largest and strongest stronghold of the white man on this globe, this matter not only concerns us, it concerns every white nation and every white person in the world. In one hundred years every person living today will be dead, or at least so feeble as not to count, which fact makes us realize that posterity will be looking back at us in a comparatively short time. If we do not stand firm now, and insure to them the same high ideals and beautiful children which our forefathers preserved inviolate for us, we shall be traitors to them.

The white race is the family of every white man on the Earth, and the man who takes the attitude that he does not care what becomes of the race after his death is too low and contemptible to be called a human being. And a man who would stand idly by and see his race mongrelized and debased during his lifetime deserves the scorn and disdain of his fellowmen.

But we cannot depend on the opinions of our very young people. They do not know enough about human nature, and a man is not competent to hold a true opinion on the affairs of mankind until he is old enough (thirty-eight or over) and learned enough to look down on popular leaders, and not up to them.

Take what is popularly called racial prejudice, for instance.

This is shouted at our young people so loud and so long that they come to believe that it is a sin; when, as a matter of fact, it means, if anything at all, love of your own race. If that is not a commendable thing, I cannot imagine anything which would be. The truth of the whole matter is that "racial prejudice" is a phrase which has been conjured up by some ignoramus who has never been capable of thinking the matter through. A man not only has the natural born right to love his own race, but since God made him a member of it, it is his moral duty to do so.

Our young people ought to be told that a white woman who goes over the line and marries a Negro commits racial suicide and becomes a traitor to her own race. She decreases the potential numbers of the white race, and adds to the potential numbers of the colored race. Her descendants will in no way be like her former family, and will forever be classed as colored. They will not have that beautiful transparent pinkness of the skin which only pure white people possess, but will be yellow skinned like the Chinese or Japanese. None of them will ever again have really lovely hair, that crowning glory of every white woman.

When one observes our children all dressed up going to Sunday School, with their hair in pretty curls which the sunlight turns into spun gold, it makes one resolve that that scene shall not pass from the world. The delicate pinkness of our young girls' skin is certainly a delight to behold. If we had nothing else to fight to maintain, that peaches-and- cream skin would be sufficient reason. And since only a white man plus a white woman can produce offspring which possess it, it is the exclusive, God-given property of the white race.

The white race does not have to assume that it is better than, or superior to, the colored race, but it must recognize, for the sake of its own preservation, the glaring truth that it is a delicate flower, which, once touched and handled by the colored race, would begin to darken, and in the end not be recognizable for the blossom it was formerly.

Knowing this, the white race is justified in taking any measures it deems necessary for its own salvation.

The Southern white man has always been right about Negroes.

It has always been his contention that if you give a Negro a foot, he will take a mile. The Southern white man has always held that Negroes and whites cannot live together on a basis of equality without the complete destruction of the white race. The people of the North, influenced by rotten, spurious literature, written by cranks and half-insane people, have professed to believe otherwise. Now they are reaping their sad reward. Negroes are demanding to be allowed to enter white society, and so bring on the disappearance of the entire white race of the world. They are too ignorant to see that the eagle is going to turn on them suddenly, and—pffft—!

CHAPTER TWO

The Illusion That Exclusion Is Abuse

Discrimination against the Negro, not only because of his color, but also because of his inborn characteristic of transmitting that color to his offspring, has been practiced by the white race since man was put on Earth. This fact is self-evident. If the white man had not battled off hordes and hordes of oncoming Asiatics and Negroes down through the centuries there would surely be no white race today. What is popularly called racial prejudice is no more than a modern expression of the natural instinct of the white man to fight for survival.

It is universally known that the Negro's color is more than skin deep; that it is in his germ cell; and that he, therefore, always transmits it to his offspring. Isn't that fact, then, sufficient reason for excluding the Negro from white society?

Which leads to a truth that is not new, and will never be old; i.e., the white man cannot allow the Negro to enter white society without the ultimate destruction of the white race. This is so obvious to any thinking man that no one in his right senses would attempt to refute it.

This is true, because if a thing is preserved on principles you cannot abolish the principles without destroying the thing they protect. Without having any written rules, the white race has preserved itself by adhering to certain tenets. One of these is: A white man or woman who marries a Negro is disgraced, and is forever ostracized from white society. The same tenet applies to a white man or woman who cohabits with a Negro without marriage.

Now, one can easily see that if the white race intends to maintain its existence, it must hold to this principle to the end of the world.

> Associate yourself with men of good quality if you esteem your own reputation; for 'tis better to be alone than in bad company.
> —*George Washington*

Once that principle dies, the race expires with it. And it is hard to see how it does any injustice to the colored peoples of the world. They can enjoy themselves among themselves as well as we can among ourselves.

Up until quite recently the Negro has been more or less content to serve the white man, and simply be a servant or entertainer at his parties. But rabble-rousers have stirred him up, and have instigated his trying to force himself right into white society. Negro leaders, the Negro press, and some trouble-making white men (whose motives are questionable) are shouting their heads off about discrimination against him on account of his color—as if that, in itself, were not reason enough.

At a meeting of the Four Freedoms Fellowship, held on March 9, 1943, in Brookline, Massachusetts, Julian Steele, president of the Boston chapter of the National Association for the Advancement of Colored People, stated that: "theories of race and racial discrimination did not come into being with Adolph Hitler." He went on to say that all over the world, in every country, white people were practicing discrimination against the Negro. He also pointed out that Massachusetts was being guided by the Jim-Crowism of the South in its policy of barring Negro doctors and nurses from the white hospitals; and that Harvard Medical School had not admitted one Negro student for the past ten years.

That organization, the National Association for the Advancement of Colored People, has been very active all over the country, trying to force our white society to permit the Negro to enter it. The leaders either do not know, or knowing, do not care, that if they succeeded the whole white race would soon disappear.

In his recent book, *Twelve Million Black Voices,* Richard Wright says that the Negro wants the "black belts" eliminated from our cities, but does not mention that that calamity would eliminate the white belts.

He states that the black belts are being eliminated, and that the Negro has crossed the line we dared him to cross. If this is true we shall have to take firm and definite action, or else we shall not survive.

Just what is it that the Negro wants from the white race? We have given him our names, we have partly civilized him, we have clothed and fed him at times, and we have permitted him to roam about at his own free will, with all kinds of ready-made opportunities for him to grasp for improving himself economically. Could we do more? Must we sacrifice our very existence for him?

Our entire civilization (social system) is built up on discriminations of one kind or another. We could all shout loud and long that we are being discriminated against. But we realize that a decent society could not exist without discriminations all along the line. The rich discriminate against the poor, and the intellectuals against the uncouth. These discriminations work for the betterment of mankind in any nation. Nearly every one of us needs someone whom we can look up to and aspire to be like; someone we can use as a model for our own development. We also need a higher standard of living to dream about and strive to reach. If we did not see people living more luxuriously than ourselves we very probably would not have any ambition stir within us. This constant striving to come up to the high living standards of others is good for us—it keeps us alive and kicking.

No one having reached the adult age of reason expects this world to be like what Heaven is supposed to be. Men are not gods, and women are far from being angels. Girls who are just plain Janes must feel that they have a right to complain about the boys discriminating against them. But do they complain? Not so you could notice it. They accept the fact of the right of the boys to pick and choose, and keep looking and hoping until they find fellows who are as plain as they.

This explains, perhaps, why so many girls with buck teeth marry fellows with buck teeth. It's the old, old story of the kettle not being able to call the pot black. It is self-protection from criticism on that sorest of points.

What has to be done to preserve and improve a people should be done by that people. Suppose that our women's dormitories did not discriminate against men! What would become of the morals of the students? Suppose that the Catholic church did not discriminate against men in a nunnery, or tolerated and sanctioned all sorts of immoral acts!

What would become of the Catholic religion?

Adults do not consider it abuse because they are excluded from children's public playgrounds. They realize that it is for the children's protection. And children do not complain that it is discrimination against them to forbid them to enter the lion's cage at the zoo. The lion himself, if he could talk, might complain that keeping him out of the rabbits' pen is unfair discrimination.

One has only to reflect on the affairs of mankind to think of thousands of instances of necessary discrimination which are required to preserve and protect society. If these discriminations are so important to uphold the morals of the white race, is it not a thousand times more important to practice a discrimination which will save that race from utter destruction?

The nature of man does not change in regard to women, and if the white man allowed colored men to get white women in their power they would take advantage of them. The white man is not so aggressive as the Negro in sex matters. Yet we do know that some white men take advantage of girls in their employ. But the tragedy in one case is not nearly so great as it is in the other. The offspring in the one case would possibly be welcomed into the world, and be adopted by some happy couple, while the offspring in the other case would be rejected by the white race, and not wanted by the colored race.

The tragedy works back to the mother also. Once a white woman crosses the color line, her conscience tells her that she is not fit to associate with white men again. It will always be so, and no law or mere government directive can change it. The reason for this is that all sane white men consider any union of a white woman with a Negro as immoral, and dog-level prostitution, no matter what kind of marriage rites may have been performed beforehand. And no rational white man will show the slightest regard or respect for a white woman who has committed this unforgivable sin. If the white man did not have this attitude there would be no white race in the space of a short time to have any kind of attitude.

Sex is a necessary evil for the purpose of propagation, and there are those who indulge in it for pleasure instead of propagation, but there are limits beyond which no white man or woman can go without sinking to levels which lead to complete moral disintegration.

There are many instances of white women having gone down, but I know of none where they came back. White men have their pride, and they had better keep it if they intend to maintain the race.

Admitting the Negro into white society would be the direst catastrophe which has ever happened to this country. No doubt it would lead to a national revolution, for we have around 80,000,000 self-respecting white people in this country who would not stand for the breaking up and degrading of our families. We may not agree on a lot of trifling questions, but on this, the question of survival, we will stand together as our forefathers did before us during the American Revolution.

An incident which took place in Cleveland recently will give some idea of the disgusting and demoralizing events which would come to pass all over the country if we permitted the Negro to enter white society. This newspaper item says that the police of that city stopped an automobile for some minor traffic violation, but since the driver, who was a Negro, had the same address as that of a club where the department had been investigating the mingling of white girls with Negro men, they decided to hold him for further questioning. Eventually they opened the trunk of his car and out tumbled the nude body of a white woman.

That kind of thing is so sickening and revolting to white men that the only consolation they can get out of it is the thought that it serves any white woman right who deserts her own race and starts

White women have been the desire of colored folk since antiquity. Here a Muslim slaver offers a beautiful white woman up for sale.

fooling around with Negroes.

Only white men really have respect for women.

Knowing the nature of man, it is not difficult to see how things would go if we started teaching our young girls that it is no disgrace to mingle with Negroes, and also invite the Negro into white society. Everybody knows how "Lucky Luciano" got our girls into his wicked clutches in New York City, and ran a string of disorderly houses.

Whether or not he had police protection, I do not remember now, but everyone knows what money will do to our police forces. Corruption and immorality are bad enough when we practice them among ourselves, but when we get the Negro mixed up into it we are not fit to be called people, but ought to be referred to as dogs. Just consider that some of our girls are continuously getting into trouble. Then is the time that they become easy prey for the underworld.

They go to a "quack" doctor to get rid of their trouble. What happens after that is a story that the police annals in any large city can readily unfold.

Yes, disorderly houses, run by Negroes, *with our girls as inmates!* If that time ever comes I sincerely hope that I am dead and in my grave long since. Think of it, and if your insides do not boil and convulse, you are not a man, but a base, perverted animal. This is not racial prejudice, whatever that is, but racial pride. We do not hate the colored race, but we love our own first. We have not yet done all we can for *our own family,* and until we lift every member of it out of the dust, it is folly and hypocrisy to pretend that we are so big-hearted that we want to lift up the colored people of the entire world. Pretty soon we are going to wake up to the fact that the colored people are very capable of forcing their way up. The Japanese are already demonstrating this.

So it is that the white man excludes the colored race from the white family for the same reason that a man excludes wolves from his lamb pen. The man who owns the lambs knows full well that if he let the wolves into the pen the lambs would soon be incorporated into the wolves, and he reflects that it is not wolves, but lambs, which he wishes to raise, therefore he excludes the wolves.

CHAPTER THREE

Why So Many Races of People?

People will not look forward to posterity,
Who are not anxious to look backward to their ancestry.
— *Edmund Burke*

Anthropologists and world historians are not in agreement in regard to the origin of the races of man. According to Dr. Ales Hrdlicka, Division of Physical Anthropology, United States National Museum, Washington, there are three main human races recognized today: i.e., white race, yellow-brown race, and the black race. But according to the late Prof. Daniel G. Brinton, American ethnologist, there are four chief groups: i.e., Caucasian, Mongolian, Malay, and Ethiopian (Negro).

Some of them maintain that the different races sprang up over the Earth as they are today, while others hold that all of them probably started from one original ancestor.

The single-ancestor school claim that man wandered over the Earth in tribes, and that climate and peculiar kinds of food gradually changed the skin and features to suit the particular locality in which a tribe happened to be isolated for a few thousand years. This school of thinkers argue that man is a product of his environment; that he will progress or regress according to the climate he lives in. The theory is that people who live in a hot, sultry climate will not put forth the necessary exertion for progress, since in most hot climates clothes are not required, and fruits and nuts offer an easily acquired food.

They point out, on the other hand, that people who live in a cold climate will find it necessary to store up food and wood for the long winter months, and that they will go a step farther and tinker with inventions to ease their labors.

This sounds reasonable enough until we reflect that the American Indian did not make any progress, either in Florida or Maine, two extremes of climate on the same continent. And the aborigines of Australia had not made any progress toward civilization when the white man found them, and have made very little since, although the climate there varies considerably, north and south.

The other school of thought gives heredity of race all the credit for progress, and discounts environment. They hold that man is capable of making his own environment, and point out what the white man did in America, Australia, and New Zealand; countries which had advanced hardly at all when discovered. The fact of the matter is, that while environment helps, good heredity plays the bigger part in the progress of a race.

Now, since the learned scholars cannot agree on one, two, or multiple races in the beginning, why cannot we adopt two as a basis for a theory, and reason it out by plain logic? We have something to work on, and shall go on from there. We all know that when a white person crosses with a Negro the resulting offspring is neither a white person nor a real Negro, but what is known as a hybrid, half-breed, or mulatto.

We also know that this mulatto has about the same skin color as the Japanese or Chinese. These mulattoes vary in feature, depending on the facial characteristics of the white race which took part in their production.

We can reason along a little further, and say that the mulatto crosses with a real Negro. Then what do we get? Still further variations in color. Or perhaps the mulatto crosses with a white person, and an entirely new and lighter hybrid is produced. Mulattoes could keep their light yellow color forever if they did not again mix with real Negroes.

Which all leads up to, and gives some basis for, my theory that in the beginning there were only two races: black and white.

Some poorly informed people seem to think that the Negro got his black skin from long continued exposure to the sun, and that a white race might become black under the same circumstances. This has been completely disproved; and here is the proof:

The pigmentation, or darkening, which a white man gets from continued exposure to the sun is only skin deep, and cannot be transmitted to his offspring. A white man may be burned almost black by the sun, but his offspring will be born just as white and pink as if he had never been in the sun. The reason for this is that a sunburn can no more affect a man's germ cell than a serious burn by fire could. He can only transmit what God put into his germ cell. If this were not true a man could transmit a bad burn caused by fire to his offspring, or in case he had a leg cut off, he might produce offspring with only one leg.

Now, since the sun never could have affected the germ cell of the Negro, we must conclude that he was created black in the beginning.

Here, then, is as good an explanation as any, of how there happen to be so many shades of color from the white man to the black man today:

The two basic races, black and white, were living in separate tribes during the early history of man. As the tribes lived mostly from hand to mouth at first, when the supply of food was exhausted in the immediate vicinity of the camp, they moved on rather than scout too far away for it. This constant moving from one place to another caused the white tribes and black tribes to meet occasionally, and war generally resulted.

In some of these conflicts, the black tribe would win, and consequently kill off all the white men, seizing their women and female children as prizes. Then, as explained above, various mixtures began to take place, with several shades of color resulting.

During this early stage of man, strength was everything, and the strongest man in a tribe ruled it with an iron hand. He naturally took all the choice women for himself. But just as surely as the brain sometimes works today to overcome brute strength, so it worked then for one of those male hybrids as he was gazing longingly at one of the attractive female hybrids. He wanted her, but he knew that the strong one had his eye on her. What to do? Like a flash it came to him! Make a run for it with her!

That he did, and unknowingly started an entirely new race.

Who can say that the Japanese and Chinese did not have this romantic beginning? Sometimes there were earthquakes, and whole mountain ranges appeared in a few hours, as the old Earth heaved and thundered!

Land appeared in the oceans where it had never been seen before, and the ocean rolled into great fissures and valleys, forming impossible spaces between the tribes. This caused our runaway boy and girl to be cut off from the black tribes for thousands of years, and consequently their descendants retained the degree of skin color which had been acquired originally. A like phenomenon may have at one time cut the black tribes off from the white tribes, making it possible for the white tribes to live in peace and make some progress toward becoming civilized. The only real evidence we have that these things must have happened is the fact that there are still white people on the Earth today, and that all colored races except the Negro appear to be a mixture.

Man's Advance from Tribal Life

When a tribe became too large for the strong man to handle single handed, he conceived the idea of appointing assistants. This was the birth of government. These deputies helped him keep order, and they formed with him the first conspiracy to force other men of the tribe to bring in their bacon as payment for being ruled. This was the birth of taxes.

Sooner or later the ruler and his deputies decided to have a separate establishment for themselves, and the strong one got himself a special wicker seat made (later to be known as the Throne) and also made himself a distinctive wreath for his head (later to be known as the Crown) so that there would be no mistake about who he was. Still later, as the ruling class grew, someone thought of the idea of forming a group of men into an organized force to repel attacks of other tribes, and also for the purpose of more efficiently keeping the population hopping along to bring in more and more bacon.

This was the birth of the army. At first the "soldiers" had only clubs as weapons, but since the population was necessarily larger than the army, and it was comparatively easy for the civilians to acquire clubs, some better weapon had to be devised. After a long time the art of forming bronze into crude blades was discovered, and the soldiers were all armed with what we now call swords. It was a simple thing for the strong man to issue a directive that no civilian should be allowed to possess them. He thus disarmed the population, and, as we all know, the population has been disarmed ever since.

The ruling class grew and grew, and a system of education (propaganda) had to be worked out, so that the civilians would feel some loyalty to their own tribe and not be running off and joining some other one. A council was formed to decide the matter, and a doctrine of loyalty to the wreath (Crown) was agreed upon. In time everything was perfected for a smooth running monarchy. Out of all this the beautiful Court of St. James grew.

In order better to maintain respect for themselves, the ruling class very early decided not to associate with the public. They agreed to marry only members of their own set, and by doing this formed the first aristocracy. This actually made a superior class of people out of them, though they did not know it, for today we are aware that inbreeding of the better class of the population produces a still higher type of man and woman. This probably accounts for the fast strides the white man's civilization took after it really got started. Tribes who advanced far enough to form any kind of government formed a monarchy. Strength has always been a factor in human affairs, and very likely always will be. The strength the strong man had has now been transferred to the police department and the army and navy. In the future a nation will very likely depend on the strength of its air force to maintain its sovereignty.

Those embryo monarchies had their troubles. Human nature was the same in those early days as it is today. Man was a jealous creature then, and he is no less jealous today. The "King" found that his own aides could not be trusted, and the best he could do was to keep the part of them who were loyal to him fighting with those who were planning his overthrow. In this, way he managed to keep his somewhat precarious seat for a number of years. The more skillful he was at playing both ends against the middle, the longer he was able to reign.

The doctrine of hereditary succession worked for the English kings for centuries. Finally, however, the people began to doubt the Heavenly appointment of the royal family, and great riots took place.

As a compromise, the king was retained, but his power over the nation was transferred to a parliament, part of which is elected by the people. Thus the English have the strongest government in the world, a democratic monarchy.

Usually when a monarchy is overthrown, the people set up a democracy, like our own. Representatives are elected by the people, and are supposed to forget their own welfare and fight for benefits for the section of the country from which they were elected. They do not always do this, however. Too often representative government descends to the level of party politics, which Pope, in 1736, defined as "the madness of many for the gain of a few," and then, as John Arbuthnot has said, "all political parties die at last of swallowing their own lies."

Other White Races

The United States has often been referred to as the melting pot of the world, but when one reflects on the matter it becomes rather obvious that the white races were fusing long before America was discovered. History teaches us how the royal families of England, France, Germany, Sweden, Italy, Norway, and so forth, married and intermarried for centuries.

Here is an extract on Sweden from *Everybody's Encyclopedia:*

"Sweden became a kingdom about the tenth century, and a little later its inhabitants accepted Christianity. It contained two races, the Swedes proper and the Goths, but after a time they were united. The early kings included St. Eric and a conqueror called Birger, and for a time the kingdom was united with Norway. In 1397 it came under the same ruler as Denmark, Finland and Norway, and for over a century there were struggles with its Danish overlords. In 1523 Gustavus Vasa succeeded in driving out the Danes, and was himself chosen king, this event marking the beginning of modern Sweden.

"In the seventeenth century Sweden, under Gustavus Adolphus and then under Charles XII, was one of the great powers of Europe, a position due chiefly to military strength. Extensive conquests were made, but they were not kept, and the rise of Russia deprived Sweden of her dominant position among the Baltic states. In 1810 Napoleon secured the choice of his marshal, Bernadotte, as heir to the childless king, Charles XIII, and in 1818 Bernadotte became king as Charles XIV. He ruled also over Norway, which was united with Sweden from 1814 to 1905. In 1907 Gustavus V, a descendant of Bernadotte, succeeded his father, Oscar II, as king."

* * *

And here is an extract from the same source, on France:

"After the conquest of Gaul by Caesar (58-51 B.C.), France, as part of the Roman Empire, took on the Roman character of its language and culture. Invaded by Vandals in the fifth century, and later by the Franks, it was ruled by Clovis. In 732 Martel led the Franks in defeating the Saracens at Tours. Charlemagne became emperor in 800. In the Middle Ages feudalism was in effect. Local barons had great power, especially in Normandy, Burgundy, and Aquitaine. In 1066 the Normans conquered England. A long Anglo-French struggle for the French crown ended in the fifteenth century."

And this extract on Germany; same source:

"For centuries 'Germany' was a loose geographical name for hundreds of states, big and little, each with its own ruler. From Otto I (A.D. 962) they owed allegiance to the head of the Holy Roman Empire, who was usually the dominant German king, but local disunion was common, especially under the feudalism of the later Middle Ages. Baltic towns became supreme in commerce; religious orders aided in expansion, and Luther's religious revolt and severe wars weakened Germany, which was dismembered in 1648, but rose again under Frederick the Great, as the kingdom of Prussia. The conquests of Napoleon ended the Holy Roman Empire in 1806."

* * *

Also this extract on Ireland; same source:

"In early times Ireland was a center of Christianity and learning, and there are still many remains of its religious houses. It was ruled by a number of kings and chiefs, who were more or less subject to a high king at Tara, and it had its own system of law, the Brehon. In the eighth century and later it suffered from the inroads of the Scandinavian pirates. Their defeat at Clontarf by Brian Boru in 1014 is regarded as a decisive event.

"In the reign of Henry II, of England, Ireland became definitely associated with England. King John, of England, called himself Lord of Ireland, and until Henry VIII took title of King, Lord was the rank of the English sovereigns there. Much land was taken from the natives and given to the English settlers, and there grew up side by side two distinct races, one dominant and land-holding, the other servile and landless.

"Later, when the Reformation had done its work, the antagonism between the two was made much worse by religious antagonism, as the Irish were Roman Catholics and the English were mainly Protestants.

"The antagonism between the two races and creeds grew steadily worse, and in the time of Queen Elizabeth it came to a head. During her reign there were constant and terrible wars in Ireland. In the end the English prevailed. In the seventeenth century, James I settled, or planted, Scotchmen in Ulster; this caused an uprising, and in 1642 there was another orgy of massacre and ruin, this time in the north. This was put down, and at the end of the civil war came the conquest of Ireland by Cromwell, another period of terror.

"The struggle between William III and James II was fought out of Ireland, and when it was over a new period of Protestant ascendancy began, which lasted for a good part of the eighteenth century. In 1750 the laws against Roman Catholics were made less severe. In 1782 Ireland was given legislative independence, but the right to vote and sit in Parliament was still confined to Protestants."

* * *

And finally this extract on Scotland; same source:

"In early days Scotland was divided into two distinct parts. The Highlands were inhabited by Gaelic tribes living in clans under their own chiefs, and the Lowlands were populated by people not unlike those living in the north of England. About 900 A.D. a king of the Scots arose.

"Governing at first only a small district in the south, and at times only a vassal of the king of England, he gradually extended his power until there was a kingdom of Scotland covering the whole of the country. Edward I conquered Scotland and made its king subject to him, but after the Battle of Bannockburn, it regained its independence, which it retained under its own kings, who were often at war with England, until 1603, when James VI became James I of

Great Britain. In 1707 the parliaments of the two countries were united and gradually the union became closer."

* * *

Need I add anything to this, to convince anyone that a white man's family is the entire white race? Each group of white people which has formed itself into what it calls a separate race picks out the rotten element in any other group (or race, if you will) and centers its fire on that, denouncing the whole race as a bunch of perjurers and murderers.

Hence, while we must fight the German army and navy to the end of this bitter family quarrel, at the same time we must not permit ourselves to hate the great German people. The people themselves are no different from thousands of decent German families now integrated into our own population. Even the boys in the army and navy are not to be blamed too much. They grew up under a dictatorial regime, where private citizens have no say but simply obey orders. Directives coming out of Washington, with that little stipulation about the $10,000 fine and imprisonment for violation, are giving us a good sample of what it means to live under one-man rule. Our own President, who is Commander-in-Chief of the Army and Navy, could find reasons for getting the Congress to declare war on Sweden, and order an attack upon that country by both the Army and the Navy. Our boys would be compelled to obey their Commander-in-Chief and make the attack, for:

Theirs not to reason why! / Theirs but to do and die!

The same is true of the German soldiers and sailors. It is not their idea, but the idea of half-insane minds at the top. It must be that the system of rounding up the insane for confinement in Germany is not efficient enough to net all who are border-line cases. It is always these half-insane, half-sane cases which are the most dangerous to be left running around loose. Everyone must know the story of Joan of Arc, who fell into the hands of the British, was found guilty of practicing sorcery, and burned at the stake.

If histories were more accurate, and the truth were told, it would probably be found that most wars are brought on by someone in authority with a streak of insanity in his make-up. Insanity and genius often travel hand-in-hand, and knowing this fact, future generations ought to look closely when they have what is popularly thought to be a genius at the head of their affairs.

This kind of thing has got to stop, or the white race will so weaken itself that it will be wiped out by the colored peoples of the world, the same as Cromwell was able to ravish Ireland during the seventeenth century after that country had been torn apart by internal wars.

Take the Italian people, for instance; they are a great people, but they have their radical fringe, which is loud and vulgar. It seems that the only Italians one hears of, except, of course, their marvellous painters and musicians, is a bunch of hoodlums who operate disorderly houses, steal automobiles, and get into trouble with the law generally.

But when one looks at a group of Italian mothers and fathers in the war pictures, one can pick out one or two who are dead images of one's own mother and father. This ought to make one hesitate to denounce all Italians.

The same is true of any white race of people. A white foreigner could steal into your house tonight and leave a deposit, and that deposit, if the truth never came out, could grow up as your own child, speak perfect English, become President of the United States, and enjoy life to the fullest. Why? Simply because his father was a white man.

The same thing could happen if the man were not a foreigner, but the lowest-down, good-for-nothing white man in America.

That is why it makes me tired when I hear some persons say that they would rather take on a Negro than such and such a white man. That good-for-nothing white tramp might produce the most beautiful girl that mankind has had the pleasure of laying eyes on, and a lovely girl is worth more than all the riches that man has piled up since he started the process.

There are those who are attempting to preach an absolutely false doctrine to us: the doctrine that we must sacrifice everything for unlimited freedom; that freedom alone will make us happy, and that having that kind of freedom is the ultimate goal of man in life. I disagree with such foolishness. What good would any kind of freedom be to me if I did not have a lovely wife and little girl to enjoy it with? And believe me, they certainly wouldn't be lovely to me if they did not have that delicious pink, translucent skin that only lily-white women possess.

Come on now, men; shout, "me too!"

While I am on this subject, I would like to suggest a way to increase our population, for we are going to need numbers in the future, and education and birth control will surely cut down our birth rate in the years to come. Here it is: Pass a Federal law that any couple producing the greatest number of children over any period of, say, five years, shall receive a check for five thousand dollars; a fund to be set up for that purpose. Then even the poorest can have hope of sudden riches. The rich won't compete, of course, but they'll have children.

A Word for and to the Jews

It is known by practically every adult and child in our Country that the Jews form one of our most talked-about minorities. Having worked for and with Jews off and on for the past sixteen years, I feel that I know a little about them. They are far from being as bad as some people are anxious to paint them to anyone who will listen, and unfortunately too many people are only too willing to listen.

The Jews are a white race, after all, and who can say that most of us don't have any Jewish mixture in us? In prehistoric days tribes overran other tribes and mixtures resulted. As I have already said, the only race of people we can be certain our folks never got mixed up with is the colored race. I don't know that my folks ever got mixed up with the Jews in tribal days, but I have had people "feel me out" before beginning a tirade against them. Then, too, I have found that I could catch right on to some of their business tricks. In fact, I became so good that I was outdoing them at their own game.

The good Jews, like the best people in our own specific race, do not lead, and do not create any disturbances which would get any publicity. Therefore you hear nothing about them, and they are the great majority. Those who are radical and noisy get all the publicity.

This fringe causes other races to curse all the Jews, the same as the Nazi leaders are now causing the whole world to curse the Germans.

Some of my own people would be surprised to meet some of the good, respectable Jews that I have known. They are absolutely no different from us. I would go to bat for them, and they would go to bat for me. You have only to know them well to like them, but they are voiceless, just like our own multitude, and nothing they say or write ever gets into print.

The radical fringe of the Jews stir up all kinds of hatred among the groups of white races and brings down the wrath of whole nations, not only on their own heads, but onto the heads of the good Jews as well. Right now, here in our country, this mob of bad Jews are doing their damndest to break down the pride we have in our ancestry and destroy our love-worship for our families. This they won't be able to do, and we resent the attempt so strongly that there is no telling what we may do if they don't soon desist.

I suppose you wonder about the devices the radical Jews use to try and kill our own self-respect, and our love and worship for our families. Here is one method: They put pictures of Joe Louis and Paul Robeson in newspapers and magazines, and praise them as being GREAT Americans. You and I get all mixed up in our thoughts. We were brought up to think that only white men could be GREAT Americans, and now look at these Negroes. Well, it just does not seem to make sense to us. We no longer take any pride in being an American; we no longer take any pride in our flag; we no longer take any pride in having made a success in our business, and we feel that we have been fooled and cheated. We reason that if these Negroes can be GREAT Americans, then we do not care to be the same. Sometimes I wonder if maybe the radical Jews in Germany did not agitate like they are agitating here right now, and that that is the reason they were turned upon.

It is this radical crowd which is stirring the Negro up, and urging him to demand to be admitted into our society. In doing this they are doing the Negro a grave injustice, for the Negro is heading for trouble, and whatever is meted out to him will also be meted out to his instigators. But these radical Jews will not take warning, for the writer knows that they have been warned many times, and know what they are doing. They must love war. Well, when it comes, they can't complain.

Refugees . . . bah!!

The best element of the Jews should form an organization and renounce all the radicals of their race who are wont to speak for them. I am sure they have no more use for their rapscallions than we have for our own.

This bad element of the Jewish people causes the good element to be ashamed of their own names, so in order to escape the stigma cast on them they go to court and throw off the label. No one can blame them for that, but for a bad Jew to take a Christian name for the sole purpose of deceiving the public should be made illegal, and severe penalties provided. I feel quite certain that the good Jews would welcome a law of this kind.

One of the worst mistakes the Jews make is the habit, when they hold meetings denouncing racial prejudice, or anti-Semitism, of tying the Negroes' case right in along with their own. This is bad, very bad, for it causes one to think and speak of Jews and Negroes in the same breath. We can absorb the Jews, and in fact are doing just that, but we cannot absorb the Negroes. The two cases are vastly different, and the sooner the Jews wake up to this fact the better it is going to be for them. Even their defense of the Negro is bad psychology—inferring that we (the gentiles) do not treat the Negro as good as they would if they were in power instead of us. The recent rioting between Jews and Negroes is evidence that the Negro does not care particularly for the Jews either. The Negro realizes that the Jews are the most self-interested race on Earth, and that consequently the Jews are being good to him only with the purpose of using him.

There is a crowd of Jews in New York who are yelling blue murder about the soldier's vote. Now those Jews are not interested in whether or not the soldier is permitted to vote. They get a malicious delight out of antagonizing, annoying, provoking, and exasperating our greatest statesmen, such as Representative John Rankin of Mississippi.

Whether Walter Winchell is a Jew or not I do not know, but he is right hand-in-glove with that cheap rabble rousing crowd. They hope through the soldier vote to put the Negro once again in control of the white people of the South. God forbid it.

Winchell, with his incessant chatter, has a great many good peo-

CHAPTER THREE | 95

Author Ira Calvin saw Walter Winchell (above) for what he was—a paid voice for Jewish interests—long before most others. Calvin insisted that Winchell was out to destroy the white race, either "consciously or unconsciously."

ple believing that he is for them, when, as a matter of fact, he is out to destroy their lovely families and magnificent homes. Why the Jergens Company makes it possible for him to invade the best homes of our country with his demoralizing line is a paradox in itself. He is out to destroy the white race, consciously or unconsciously, and as Jergens lotion would be of no earthly use to mulattoes, it is hard to understand why a company would employ a man to hasten its own ruin and downfall. Common sense tells us that when you advertise a lotion to keep hands white and beautiful you are not addressing that advertisement to Negroes and mulattoes. We all know that their hands are neither white nor beautiful, and Jergens lotion would not make them so; nor would any other lotion for that matter.

You will notice that Winchell never says anything against the radicals and communists. He likes to harp at what he calls fascists.

And bear this in mind . . . you are a fascist, yourself, according to him, if you believe that you have a right to say with whom your children will associate, and also that you have a right not to employ any man who might be a detriment to your business or family. He is for making you and me bow down to anti-discrimination laws, whether it would mean the extinction of our families or not. He is always shouting about freedom of the press . . . now let him defend my right to say what I am saying about him.

CHAPTER FOUR

Civilization Versus Barbarism

> Can the Ethiopian change his skin, or the leopard his spots?
> —*Jeremiah XIII: 23*

One might say that civilization is the opposite of barbarism. But it is not so simple as that. *Everybody's Complete Encyclopedia* says that it is:

> A stage of cultural development of human society. At first serving to distinguish generally the higher states from those of savagery and barbarism. The intensive study of human origins introduced new lines of demarkation. The starting point of civilization is nowadays usually associated with one or the other primary invention, such as pottery, writing, metallurgy, or the domestication of animals or of plants. But prehistoric periods are recognized as having had their social states also, and one may therefore speak of the stone age, bronze age, or early iron age of civilization.

Ordinarily we speak of a people as being civilized, half-civilized, or savage. The American Indian was certainly a savage when the white man found him, and the Negro slaves the white man brought with him were little more than docile barbarians. The making of and using a spear surely does not make a savage civilized, nor does the making of and using a machine gun make the Japanese any more so.

Starting in the north of Europe, the white man has pushed civilization down through that continent to England, then across the Atlantic to America, to Australia and New Zealand. How the white man conquered this continent, and pushed civilization westward, tree by tree, under the constant, murderous eye of the savage from the ambush makes interesting reading.

As James Truslow Adams points out in his book, *The Epic of America*, "the finger of fate beckons, and the white man is powerless to resist it." Always looking for new territory to tame, he now finds that all the land on this globe is staked and claimed, so he will have to set about improving it instead of exploring it.

What he did find was that there are vast areas of land heavily populated by half-civilized people who have a peculiar yellow skin.

He soon learned that they had certain products which he wanted, so he offered to trade with them, and when they refused he went away, but later came back with men and guns and moved in on them. He contrived to enlist the help of some of the more friendly ones, and after a time was able to set up a colony. Thus began what is called the white man's imperialism.

This imperialism has been far more beneficial to these colored peoples than many persons seem to realize. They observed the white man's clothes, and began to discard the traditional loin cloth. They watched his behavior and started to imitate him. But there was one thing they could not understand nor imitate, and that was the art of

CHAPTER FOUR | 99

play which the white man indulged in. Even today the colored people of the world do not go in for such things as motor boating, hunting, fishing, and a multitude of other sports which the white man loves just for the fun there is in them.

It is remarkable how slowly these colored races have responded to the civilizing process. Some of them, after all the centuries which have passed since they first saw the white man, still do not wear decent clothes. The women do not even cover their breasts, but leave them exposed to the world. Possibly the reason for this is that they are black, or deep brown, and they know that no one is interested in looking at them anyway. This leads one to reflect that maybe clothes never would have been invented had there been no white women in the world.

The mass of people in India, China, and Japan (all colored races) are only half-civilized at this late day, and that fact makes one wonder whether or not they will ever be wholly civilized. Which leads to the question: Can a colored people have an advanced stage of civilization thrust upon them?

The sudden and brutal attack by the Japanese on Pearl Harbor would seem to indicate that it cannot. They, with their machine guns and aeroplanes, are definitely demonstrating what it leads to when you put such instruments into the hands of superficially civilized persons.

The frequent raping and murdering of white girls by Negroes, also brings one to the conclusion that they are only outwardly civilized.

An article in the March (1942) issue of *Photo-Story* by Major Malcolm Wheeler-Nicholson, British Liaison and Intelligence Officer to the Japanese General Staff in Siberia in 1918, gives some vivid accounts of Japanese torture of helpless human beings and animals. In one instance, he says he saw the soldiers using a live horse for sword practice. They had the horse strung up over the limb of a tree so that its front feet were off the ground, and one of its front legs was hanging limp and twisted, indicating that it had been shattered. A Japanese soldier swung his sword and cut a great hunk from the poor animal's rump. It hung down bleeding and quivering. The Jap swung again, and cut it off with dexterity and skill. The other soldiers shouted with glee.

In another instance he saw the Japanese dog catchers dragging their victims along behind them by ropes, after they had mercilessly broken the animals' hind legs.

Later on he came across some Japanese soldiers dragging five Russian prisoners. Ropes were around their necks, and they were moaning so distressingly that he stopped the soldiers and made inquiry.

It came out that the soldiers had stopped to boil rice and make some tea, and to make sure that the prisoners would not get away they had dropped the heavy gun butts on their feet, breaking their insteps—thus applying the technique of the dog catchers to human beings.

It was while he was on his way to Vladivostok that he saw a torture case that convinced him that the Japanese officers are no more human than the most ignorant peasant. His train had stopped at a station called Vasiljeva, on the Bilkin River. He and his associate Russian liaison officer, Cossack Lieutenant Alexieff, walked down on to the platform to look around before the train pulled out.

The uproar of a crowd at the rear of the station attracted their attention. They started toward the mob, and when the peasants saw the officers they dispersed quickly, leaving behind a bloody wreck of a man. Let Mr. Nicholson describe what had been done to him: "His ears had been sliced off, his nose was a blood-smeared mess, his toes had been chopped off, his hands showed only the bleeding stumps where his fingers had been. His eyes were blackened holes. An unspeakable offence, too, had been committed upon his person. He still lived, moaning in that animal-like fashion."

Mr. Nicholson's associate, Alexieff, reached for his revolver and put the miserable human out of his misery.

The station master came out of hiding and told Alexieff that the man had been a Russian civil engineer. He had been arrested by the Japanese on some pretext in Khabarovsk, and was being taken to headquarters in Vladivostok, when one of the Japanese guards had purposely burned him with a lighted cigarette. He had responded by knocking the guard down. The Japanese officer in charge halted the train at this station, and had his men commit each separate torture upon the helpless man. After they had satisfied their anger upon him they flung his bleeding body onto the loading platform. That officer was a Lieutenant Sakae Minamoto, a military police officer, stationed in Siberia.

Another incident which Mr. Nicholson tells about happened near Spasskoi while he was out with a mounted patrol from his regiment, the Twenty-Seventh Infantry. The howling of a dog had attracted their attention to a deserted farmhouse. There was no sign of life about the place, except the poor, lonely dog, which slunk away. Something on the barn door made them curious, and they discovered that it was the body of a young baby pinned there by a Japanese bayonet. This made them wonder what had become of the young parents, so they made a search, and found the mother's nude body under some leaves. She apparently had been mass raped, and tortured with bayonets. Then they found the father, who had been buried alive, both his arms having been broken. The Japs had buried him in such a way that his head was above the ground, so that he could witness the brutal raping and murdering of his wife.

All these things caused Major Nicholson to declare that, "The

Japs, in spite of their superficial civilization, have always been barbarians, and always will be barbarians."

It is becoming more and more clear to the white man that monkey can see and monkey can do, without becoming really civilized.

Our civilization is built up on what are called inhibitions. The white race has developed these inhibitions for thousands of years, and now it is very easy for a white person to refrain from doing what he would like to do but knows will injure someone else. You can make a white man angry, but he is not apt to kill you or have you tortured, as Lt. Sakae Minamoto did to the victim as related. The inhibitions of the white man remove him farthest away from the jungle. He does not fall back into his jungle ways so quickly and completely upon becoming angry as do the colored races.

According to the anthropologists, it has taken the white man many thousands of years to develop to his present state since he first learned to coordinate his hands with his brain. But it must be plain to any thinking person that only the white race really made substantial progress toward higher civilization after that initial step. When the white man discovered this continent, he found the Indian in the Neolithic stage, and it is probable that he would still be in it had the white man not come. It is safe to say that the Indian has advanced more during the few hundred years since the white man came than he did during thousands of years prior to that event. The same thing is true of the Negro. But, as already stated, since civilization is not to be instilled into savages in a few centuries, their civilization is all on the surface. Anger, or sexual passion throw them right back into the jungle state.

The Japanese was the first colored race to turn on the white race. According to an *Associated Press* dispatch of June 9, 1943, Tadahiko Okada, speaker of the Japanese House of Representatives, said:

Japan must utterly destroy the United States and Great Britain or be destroyed herself. The grim nature of this global war will permit no half-baked distinction between victor and vanquished. It is a question of the survival of the fittest—eat or be eaten. There is absolutely no room for the co-existence of Japan on the one side, and Britain and the United States on the other. We must crush and overthrow those two countries which are cruelty and craftiness incarnate. The United States is attempting to control Europe across the Atlantic and East Asia across the Pacific in an outspoken action of extreme imperialism.

It is fortunate for the white man that they are not quite civilized enough to realize that they are not his equals, and that mere brutality cannot stand against intelligence and a scientific plan in warfare. The white man has far more to fight for than any colored race. His very existence depends on his ability to ward off attack. It has always been so, and always will be so, for while the white man is perfectly content to allow the colored races to live in peace as long as they do not butt into his family (the white race), he knows, or ought to know, that if the colored races ever came to power they would wipe him out for safety.

What the Colored Race Wants

While some of our leaders are talking about a planned *world*, here at home we are not planning our future at all. While they talk glibly of a quart of milk a day for *everyone* in the *whole world*, people are *forced to freeze* in sub-zero weather in New England, because no one had brains enough to size up local conditions, much less appraise the troubles of this entire planet. It simply does not make sense, and is a serious symptom that there is something *radically wrong* with our method of electing our representatives.

Have we let a ridiculous and unworkable sentimentality grow upon us? How long can we remain fools and still survive? Shall we ever wake up and realize that the colored races do not, and cannot be taught to, think kindly toward mankind as we do? The reason for this is that it is easy to regard the underdog with a certain pity, but the underdog not only resents the patronage but will strive forever to turn the tables.

If the white man ever relaxes enough for the tables to be turned, he will disappear from the face of the Earth.

The white man has the one thing which makes this life worth living at all, and that is his beautiful women. He idolizes woman from the cradle to the grave. She causes him to build large corporations, to construct canals, to build railroads; in fact, everything worthwhile he does is on her account. If it wasn't for her beautiful skin, which invites adornment to make it all the more luscious, the white man would still be in the jungle eating nuts and berries. But sometime in the dim past he must have taken a close look at that Dresden china skin and mumbled something like, "Mmmn, this jungle ain't no place for a lady—I must get a leopard skin or something to cover her up before some of those other cave men get ideas."

One of that cave man's descendants, who happens to be King Edward VIII of England, thought so much of that peaches-and-cream skin that he sacrificed his throne to possess it.

It is known by almost every adult person that among all the colored races, however slight their pigmentation, the men rule with an iron hand, and the women are no more than slaves. Now, any aggression the colored races take towards the white man is wholly by the men of those races, and not by the women.

Men don't wage war for nothing, and therefore we must have

something which the Japanese want for themselves. They don't need our wealth. They don't need our territory, and they have plenty of fisheries. They cannot possibly claim that we have them bottled up and encircled as the Germans do. From what information I can get, they had free range of the seas before this war, just like any other nation.

And we were doing quite a business with them; too much business in scrap iron, as it turned out. What, then, can they want from us? Could it be our lovely women?

White men haven't protected and preserved the delicate whiteness of their women's skins these thousands of years to wind up by handing them over to the colored races to despoil.

They will die first!

They know that they would have nothing left to live for. Wealth and freedom would not mean a thing to a white man if he had no lovely lady to share it with. The fact of the matter is that the civilization we have has been built up by the white man to please his women, and induce them to admire him for being so smart.

What do we men and women back here at home think that our boys are fighting for? They are fighting mainly to preserve our liberty, but they are also fighting to protect their sweethearts, their wives, and their mothers and sisters from ever becoming contaminated with any kind of colored blood. Our boys are not fighting to establish any new freedom that would eventually lead to complete dissolution of the white race. They realize that slavery under a white man would be preferable to seeing our girls bossed even in the slightest degree by a colored man. I'll say it now, and I'll say it again later on, that colored men have no right to expect white men to allow them to be over friendly with white girls. We know human nature too well for that.

It has been reported that many of the Japanese prisoners of war can speak perfect English, and are acquainted with the names and lives of most of our beautiful movie and stage actresses. This would indicate that those who we have permitted to study at our colleges are now using our brilliant teaching to defeat our tactics and destroy more of our own boys. This should be a lesson to us. We can never instill our ideals into any colored race, and the sooner we get this fact into our heads, the better. The danger in trying to change other people is that in the process you, yourself, might become changed over to their low ideals.

Wrong and futile thinking has steered us off our course, but it is not too late yet to take our bearings and tack about. By changing our course now we can avoid untold bloodshed later. A government may compel its people to do what is against its will and grain for a time, but sooner or later revolt will set in, and then what could have been settled by peaceful means is accomplished "by the sword."

CHAPTER FIVE

Our Deluded Leaders

You can fool some of the people all of the time, and you can fool all of the people some of the time, but you can't fool all of the people all of the time.

—*Abraham Lincoln*

If it be treason to advocate the overthrow of the government of a people, it follows, as truly as the fact that the whole is greater than any of its parts, that to advocate the destruction of the people themselves is the highest kind of treason. Whoever in any way contrives to get the Negro into white society is guilty, either consciously or unconsciously, of advocating the destruction, not only of the white people of that particular country, but of the entire white race. Any man who accepts public office must expect that, sooner or later, the spotlight is bound to be thrown on his doings. As Swift says, "Censure is the tax a man pays to the public for being eminent." Up until now these men have apparently been quite proud of their actions, but any man or woman who cannot see that the entrance of the Negro into white society would eventually destroy that society, is void of reason, and should not be permitted to hold public office.

I have here some clippings from magazines and newspapers which I have gathered during the past year. These items have been published throughout the country, but being aware of the fact that not all my fellow white citizens have been in a position to buy and read the numerous periodicals and newspapers published, in order to secure all this information, I shall now recount them here.

I have heard some people say that we should not believe what we see in the newspapers, but it is my opinion that they usually print the truth. Any newspaper that lost the confidence of the public in this serious matter would soon find its circulation down to nothing. It is hard to see how a publication could justify its existence if it did not print the exact facts. Since no one is compelled by law either to buy or read any certain newspaper, and therefore one acts of one's own accord, it follows that the approval of the public is necessary for the very existence of any one of them. This being the case, it ought to be safe to assume that what a newspaper prints is very likely to be authentic.

But I will say, while upon this subject, that the majority of the legitimate newspapers and magazines of this country have entirely failed in their obvious duty to the majority to enlighten the American people to just what has been going on as far as race relations between the white people and the colored people are concerned. Their policy has evidently been to avoid controversial issues, and since their continued prosperity depends on such a policy as regards most "hot" issues, one is apt to side with them. However, when the issue at stake concerns the very existence of a man's own family, and in a larger sense, his whole race, it certainly seems to be time for him to throw overboard any policy which conflicts with his ideals, and "spill the beans." His bread and butter surely are not more important than the continued existence of his own family. When a man ceases to be a man, and refrains from shouting "fire" when he sees his own house burning down, because of fear of loss of mere money, he really ought to do his race one last favour and go off and die somewhere. It would be more honorable than sitting and "fiddling." "Sitting this one out" is not going to be either honourable or safe. Records are being kept of every man's actions in this crisis of the white race.

A newspaper has just been delivered at my office, and I see here on the front page an article telling about the delinquency in Boston among our 'teen-age girls. According to police reports, there has been a forty per cent rise in the number of girls brought before the Juvenile Court. The number of runaway girls has shot up 400 per cent over 1941. There is four times as much truancy, and there are twice as many cases of sex violations. And here is the last sickening fact: the average age of the girls arrested is just fifteen! Now, our leaders would not even dream that they are very largely responsible for this terrible breakdown in the moral standards of our young girls. But I shall attempt to show how this has been done. Constantly tell the young of any nation that they are no better than half-civilized savages, and in time they will come to believe it, and act accordingly. Which leads us to our first public official.

Speaking in Chile, Vice-President Henry A. Wallace made this statement: "We children of the United States are not a superior race, and the Nazis are not either."

Now, what does that mean? It means that a man to whom our children look up to more than they do to us has told them that they are no better than those subhuman, bestial Japs. It means that our children are told that pride and dignity and love of family and race are wrong, and that anyone who advocates these things is a Nazi. It means that our children are indoctrinated with the idea that pride of ancestry is old fashioned, and that in order to be smart they must break with every tradition that the white race has built up for its own advancement and preservation. That such teaching as this is already showing dire results should not surprise any sensible man or woman.

Now about Mr. Wendell Willkie: Practically everyone knows by now just what he advocates. He has written a book called *One World*, and I suppose he also proposes "one people," but it is a fact that he is completely out of touch with the ordinary man. Here before me I have a picture of him sitting very close to that Negro torch and blues singer, Lena Horne. From the intimate way in which he and she are talking, one gathers the impression that he is enjoying the experience. Wonder if he thought of the fact that all decent white girls would forever after that scorn the chance to sit by him. It would certainly be no honor to them. Reason is reason, and there is no denying that once a white person associates with Negroes he is not only held in contempt by white people but is despised by the Negroes themselves.

And now for Mrs. Eleanor Roosevelt: Hardly a person in these United States is in the least doubt about where she stands on this issue. Her case clearly illustrates what I just stated in the above paragraph.

The Negroes are now calling her by her first name in their press. Think of that—the President's wife deserving so little respect that the Negroes are getting chummy enough with her to call her just plain Eleanor! If that is not a national disgrace, I am at a loss to think of anything which would be. One can bet that when she started this business she did not realize that the whole Nation would lose respect for her, and that Negro kitchen women would form "Eleanor" clubs.

Harold L. Ickes was a confidant of FDR and Eleanor and a champion of rights for the black man in America.

Next comes Harold L. Ickes: In a magazine which I have before me I am perusing an article which says that President Roosevelt, Mrs. Roosevelt, and Ickes are the three persons most responsible for the rise in the status of the Negroes. It goes on to tell how Ickes hired many Negroes for the PWA, and how he compelled the white employees to work right with them in the various offices, or resign. Not satisfied to stop there, he went with a group of them to a municipal golf course which had always been reserved for white people, and rounded up some park policemen "to enforce the order"—but where such an order came from it does not say—that they might play, in spite of any objection by the white golfers. That kind of action is not legitimate in a country where the "will of the majority is law." Mr. Ickes has certainly been riding high and mighty over the American people, but pretty soon now he will be relegated to the graveyard. That is one good thing about "time"—it discards tyrants in the same manner as it does the poorest beggar.

Since President Roosevelt has insisted during his entire reign on ordering everybody beneath him to do his bidding, he will have to accept the blame for some things which have been done which smell to the high heavens. Take that pamphlet *The Races of Mankind*, for instance. That pamphlet, and the motives behind it, will go down in history as a blot on the present Administration. If you are a decent person you will need a clothes pin on your nose while you study it, for it stinks. Imagine trying to convince sensible white people that they are no different from Negroes, Japanese, Chinese, and Indians. You might just as well try to convince them that day is no different from night, or black no different from white. Our Army made arrangements to purchase fifty thousand of these spurious pamphlets to hand out to your boy and mine. Fortunately out of over five hundred men representing us in the two Houses of Congress we had one man there, Rep. Andrew J. May, Democrat from Kentucky, who stood up and denounced that pamphlet and the motives behind it. Said he: "It won't be distributed by the Army. If it is, we will have plenty to say and it will be said right on the floor of the House. It has no place in the Army program."

If you needed a clothes pin on your nose to read the pamphlet described above, you'll need a gas mask to read one called *Common Ground*, which was distributed to the Junior Hostesses at Service Canteens in New York City. It advises white girls at the canteens that they had just as well get down off their high horses and dance with Negro soldiers. It apparently was written by one Margaret Halsey (we'll want to remember her name) and is an attempt to convince

Liberal Franklin Delano Roosevelt and his ultra-liberal wife, Eleanor, take a presidential ride. Together, the Roosevelts forged a socialistic American welfare state that would have made Karl Marx and Friedrich Engles grin from ear to ear.

our girls that with rapid means of transportation after this war they will not be able to get away from the Negroes, and had just as well begin now to make love to them. It is one of those disgusting things that have appeared lately, and those in the White House must be sanctioning them, for if they were not who would dare put out such stuff? The drive being waged to destroy the white race is amazing in that some white persons are practically leading it.

How did a person with the mind of this Halsey woman ever get into a position of authority at those Canteens? I'll tell you that we are certainly on the road to destruction if we do not call a halt. She has a helluva nerve, telling our girls that because of the rapid rise of machinery we have lost control of our destiny. We'll show her, and a lot of other people, that we have not by any means lost our perspective.

Unless what I have said, or might say, about communists in New

York should cause some people to link Governor Thomas E. Dewey right in with them, I want to state here and now that he is not even a New Yorker. He was brought up in a small town, the same as I was (we're about the same age) and the big city will never distort his vision any more than it will mine. There in New York he stands like a stonewall against a multitude of Negroes and white communists.

The whole country knows his good record. As District Attorney of New York County, he challenged organized and entrenched vice, and won. It was he who put down Lucky Luciano with his string of disorderly houses, and routed vice in general from high places.

His latest feat was the defeat of two anti-discrimination bills put in by communists, and designed to make it illegal for white people to refuse to hire Negroes. The story of how Governor Dewey got around letting those two atrocious bills become law makes enlightening reading.

He deserves credit from the decent people of the whole State, in fact, of the white people of the whole country. If you are interested in which side of the fence he is on, just notice what groups are attacking him.

CHAPTER SIX

Newspaper Clippings & Comments

A free and courageous press is part of the heritage of every American.... Without complete and accurate information on the activities of the Government, on the state of the Nation, and on the outside world, he cannot offer intelligent criticism or poll an intelligent vote.

—*Neil MacNeil* from *Without Fear or Favor*

A free press, a free people; a controlled press, a slave people. The Negro press has been slugging right and left to force legislation to make it illegal for white people to refuse to admit Negroes to our hotels, our swimming pools, our churches, our schools, our private parties, or to mention that we want only white persons to apply when we are advertising for help. That press, and the National Association for the Advancement of Colored People also want legislation forbidding white newspapers from mentioning that the criminal in a rape case was a Negro, if such was in fact the truth. Talk about aggressiveness, these people want the legal right to force their way in, and if they get it you will see scenes which will make you shed tears of blood!

Here are actual headlines from white and Negro newspapers:

* * *

OCT. 1—RACE BIAS GETS SENATE BACKING

This is the story of how the Senate voted on the Price Control Bill. Amendments regarding discrimination in hiring personnel for the price, rent, and rationing boards had been offered. One offered by Senator Alexander Wiley (Republican), from Wisconsin, provided that: There shall be no discrimination in the administration of the benefits of the Emergency Price Control Act, on account of race, creed, or color in the membership of rent, price, and rationing boards.

Another one of our deluded leaders! His electors ought to remember this when he comes up for reelection. Why men from states where there are very few Negroes or foreigners are forever putting amendments to bills in their favor, defies psychological explanation. It seems strange that they are more interested in the problems of other sections of the country than they are in their own.

* * *

OCT. 4—SENATE COMMITTEE BALKS ON ANTI-POLL TAX BILL

In this case, a Senator from the South, who ought to know better, introduced the bill. He is Claude Pepper, from Florida. This bill would ban the small fee paid as a poll tax as a prerequisite for voting.

It would put the power to elect national officials in the hands of ignorant Negroes, and whites who don't even read a newspaper, and consequently would lead to the election of any crooked crackpot who happened to have a good line to hand out over the radio. People who do not pay a poll tax certainly do not pay any other kind of taxes, and one wonders just what good they are to a state. Those states down there might follow the example of highly enlightened Massachusetts, and send out constables to arrest the poor wretches for not paying their poll taxes on time, and also add on outrageous charges which are sometimes many times the tax itself.

Since Massachusetts compels every adult man to pay the poll tax, or be jailed, it might just as well let the men think they are getting something for their money by reserving the right to vote for those who pay on time. Making everyone pay without offering anything in return looks to the casual observer as a species of legalized robbery.

When we consider that those on the welfare, in a lot of cases just able-bodied idlers, are not required to pay the tax—which, after all, would be absurd, since the money they get is the collections themselves—but are allowed to vote, it appears that the industrious and thrifty are suffering extra taxation but are not given any extra representation.

However, when our great national Government stops motorists on the road, and says, "Listen, you; up to now you have had a natural right to drive your car on this highway, because of your having complied with certain regulations; but all that is over; we are taking away that right, here and now; you either hand over a five dollar bill or you don't drive another step,"—it is small wonder that taxes are levied against the citizen by individual States without any semblance of return therefore. Believe it or not, there are a cheap lot of ward politicians in every large city who depend on the welfare votes for their election. Imagine letting the feeble minded vote!

* * *

OCT. 26—APPEAL TO F.D.R. IN LYNCHINGS

Negroes in Harlem held a protest meeting at which the lynching of two colored boys of eighteen in Mississippi was denounced. The National Negro Congress sponsored the meeting, and wires which had been sent to Governor Johnson asking for a Grand Jury investigation were applauded. A wire had been sent the President also, requesting him to instruct the Attorney General's office to use its investigating powers granted by the Civil Rights Act.

Imagine that! They want the Federal Government to butt into States' affairs. They do not seem to realize that once a precedent is set, it might be followed up to their own detriment when Mr. Roosevelt is no longer in the driver's seat.

* * *

OCT. 28—AUTONOMY TIFF WON BY FEPC

As everyone ought to know by now, the Fair Employment Practices Act was never passed on by the Congress, and consequently could hardly be called a law. The Constitution plainly and solemnly states that the Congress shall make the laws. In this case the President simply went right over the head of Congress, and issued an executive directive to the effect that a man can no longer say whom he will hire, but must take all who apply, if there is work that they can do.

This directive was so against the grain of the independent and intelligent American people that it struck snags at every turn. The Negro associations were right on their toes to get every man arrested who refused to hire Negro men to work right alongside white women. It appears to me that in a matter that would change our entire social setup, and very probably eliminate all white people in time, even the Congress itself has no power to act, but the question ought to be put up to the people themselves. Congress would do well to consider such a law, reserving to the people the right to pass on such far-reaching legislation.

* * *

OCT. 28—F.D.R. SAYS HIS VIEWS CONCUR WITH WILLKIE'S

The President says that he agrees with Willkie that men and nations must have more freedom after the war.

It is hard to understand in what way men want more freedom.

No new freedom will come out of this war. Men will not be free to plunder and ravage other men's homes and women. No society will ever grant one man the right to force his presence upon that of another when he is not wanted. One race of people will never get the right to force itself on another race and destroy it.

* * *

OCT. 28—SOUTHERN SENATORS GANG UP TO TALK POLL TAX TO DEATH

Twelve Southern Senators prepare a filibuster to prevent the Pepper-Geyer Anti-Poll Tax measure from coming to a vote on the floor. Senator Thomas Connally of Texas and Senator Theodore Gilmore Bilbo of Mississippi can be credited with keeping the rotten element from some of our Northern cities from having their way. The way they stood their ground, and fought like warriors of old to save not only the white people of this Nation, but the white people all over the world, from eventually falling under the rule of the colored races, will go down in history as a tribute to their valor. The odds against them were tremendous, but when men really have something to fight for their passion and ardor rise with the occasion and they stick to their guns with a vengeance.

Right after the Civil War the white people of the South were put in worse chains than the Negroes who had been freed had ever experienced. A vicious element of white men were sent down there from the North, and they put Negroes over the white people. It must have been a disgrace for this country in the eyes of the rest of the white world. Black congresses were formed, and a black bunch of representatives sent to our National Capitol to enact legislation. One can imagine that that legislation was entirely favorable to the Negroes themselves. But as no man, or group of men, can keep the cream from rising to the top, the white people of the South gradually got control of their government back into their own hands. Had they failed to do this, even after their back had been broken and their pride ground in the dust, it is entirely possible that there would not be a real white person in the South today. Indeed, when you consider the aggressiveness of the Negroes, it is more than likely that there would not be a real white person in the entire United States.

* * *

NOV. 21—NEGRO CONFERENCE OUTLINES POLICY

The New York State Conference of Negro Youth held a meeting in Harlem and drew up a policy declaring that the treatment of Negro youth in the United States is a yardstick of Democracy. A Chinaman by the name of Liu Liang-Mo spoke and said that the Chinese are a colored race also. He pointed out that the Chinese deplore lynchings, and stated that their newspapers here and in China are denouncing the poll tax filibuster. Well!

Nov. 21—ALABAMA RACE HATRED HALTS NEGRO TRAINING

These Northern newspapers will not see that the Southern people do not hate the Negroes. It is for the survival of the white race that they are fighting.

* * *

NOV. 23—NEGROES SUE TO COMPEL CLEVELAND WAR FACTORIES TO GIVE THEM JOBS

Did I say these people are aggressive?

* * *

Nov. 25—WHITE TRASHER HAILS LOLLIPOPS

This item calls Representative John E. Rankin of Mississippi "white trash." I don't see how they get away with such talk. Anyway the Negroes are very handy with that phrase, and it will likely be their undoing when white men realize that a man's first duty is to his own family. A white man's family is the white race, and when he ignores the suffering and poverty in his own, and bestows his love and affection on the colored family, he is indeed a strange and despicable creature.

Dec. 11—RANKIN BLASTS AGAINST FEPC

More about the Fair Employment Practices Committee. Here again Representative Rankin is called "white trash," and accused of raving about the order of the Committee directing the Capital Transit Company of the District of Columbia to discontinue discrimination against Negroes in its hiring of bus and trolley car operators. Representative Rankin said that such an order, throwing Negroes right into white society, is fanning the flame of race hatred.

He mentioned a similar order which had been given to the Delta Shipbuilding Corporation of New Orleans, and pointed out that the Montgomery Ward Company had been ordered to bow down and permit the labor agitators of the CIO to dictate its policy.

* * *

JAN. 6—NEGRO DENIED SECOND DRAFT WRIT

The case of Winfred Lynn, a Jamaica Negro. The American Civil Liberties Union appealed his case, saying that the manner in which he had been inducted into the army was discriminatory. The Judge explained the quota system and denied the writ.

* * *

JAN. 23—FEPC FRIENDS KEEP UP FIGHT

Trying to bring it back to life. They won't believe that this Dictator law cannot work here.

* * *

FEB. 1—ANTI-NEGRO BIAS CHARGED TO AIR COMMAND

Judge William H. Hastie, Negro adviser on Negro problems, to secretary of War Henry L. Stimson, resigns in protest against what he terms "reactionary policies and discriminatory practices" within the Army Air Force Command.

* * *

MARCH 11—NEGRO EXTRADITED TO MISSISSIPPI

One George Burrows, a Negro, was being taken back to Mississippi to answer charges of asking a white girl to kiss him and for shooting two white men. He had fled to New York. The Negro told the Judge that he was in fear of being lynched in the Southern State.

* * *

MARCH 23—TREAT ALL RACES AS EQUALS TO GET REAL WORLD PEACE

From one of Mrs. Roosevelt's columns. She does not see that the colored races would soon lord it over the white race if the time ever came when they had the numbers and power. There never can be an equality between the two races; either one or the other will be supreme.

If the white race surrenders its supremacy, it will at the same time surrender its very existence. The dullest moron will not have to tax his brain to see this truth.

* * *

MARCH 26—RANKIN RENEWS RACIAL TIRADE

John Rankin is the greatest man in the House of Representatives today. He fights not only for the white people of this country, but for the white people the world over. He is the only man who realizes how quickly the white race would be wiped off the face of the Earth if we lost control here in the United States, the major stronghold of the white man on this globe.

* * *

MARCH 25—MARTINIQUE NEGROES THREATEN REBELLION

Even on the islands they are getting stirred up!

* * *

MARCH 12—CONNECTICUT ACTS ON BIAS

Getting somewhere, aren't they?

* * *

APRIL 2—JOB DISCRIMINATION GOES ON AS FEPC REMAINS DORMANT

A separate State is the answer.

APRIL 2—NMU TELLS OF WINNING FIGHT ON JIM CROWISM

The National Martime Union issued a pamphlet telling how the Negro is forcing his way into jobs on ships which have had an all-white policy up to now. It points to specific cases of employers who resorted to every trick to avoid hiring Negroes. How far all this can go before a violent reaction sets in is a question to think about.

* * *

APRIL 9—DOWNEY ASSAILS JIM CROW

Senator Sheridan Downey of California called on the Senate to investigate discrimination against Negroes in the armed services. His electors might remember this when he comes up for re-election.

* * *

APRIL 13—BAR ASSOCIATION PROBED ON CHARGE OF BANNING NEGRO

Maybe they'll start to admit them now!

* * *

FEB. 19—TWENTY-FOUR HOUSING PROJECTS HAVE WHITE, NEGRO TENANTS

This one really caps the stack. Imagine whites living in the same building with Negroes, and Washington announcing it with pride!

Such a thing as that may be the beginning of the disappearance of the white man. Can those white tenants have any love for their daughters, or any regard for their descendants? They ought to remember that our great South and West are not going to follow them if they go over to the colored side.

* * *

APRIL 19—WHITE TENANTS OPPOSE BAN BY NEGRO LANDLORD

This headline is somewhat misleading. A Negro bought a building, and gave all the white tenants notice to find other quarters. He said that he had learned from the experiences of other landlords that it was not advisable to have both races in the same building. He also said that he was not interested in social experimentation.

* * *

APRIL 24—NO LIKEE MIXEE. SCHOOL HEAD QUITS

The Cheltenham School for Boys, seventy-five miles from Baltimore, is involved in this case. The school board has five Negro members, and it voted to institute joint living and eating quarters for the colored and white employes. This caused John H. Blandford, member for twenty-six years, and president for five, to resign. Blandford is a strict segregationist. After he turned in his resignation, twenty-one white employes threatened to quit.

* * *

APRIL 24—SNATCHES BREECHES OFF WHITE DURHAM POLICE

Some Negro soldiers got into a scuffle with the Durham, North Carolina, police, and succeeded in pulling off the pants of a couple of them. This kind of thing hasn't even happened in the North yet.

* * *

APRIL 24—HOUSE PETITIONED TO FIGHT JIM CROW

The New York Legislature has petitioned the Congress to enact legislation giving the FEPC full power of investigation, subpoena, prosecution, and enforcement, together with substantial funds to carry out its purpose. Looks as if they want to get all the white people put in jail.

* * *

APRIL 24—SUIT TO ENTER KENTUCY UNIVERSITY SET

The National Association for the Advancement of Colored People, representing one Charles Lemont Eubanks, has filed suit to force the University to admit him, and to recover $5600 in damages from the registrar for the year he has not been a student. There is a State law which prohibits a Negro from being admitted to a white college, and there is a Kentucky State College for Negroes at Frankfort.

* * *

MAY 7—BILL LIMITS ADVERTISEMENTS FOR JOBS

What won't they think of next? This bill was filed on petition of Rabbi Joseph S. Shubow in the Massachusetts Legislature. It would prohibit a man or woman from stating in an advertisement for household help that he or she wanted only white people to apply. As I said before, if we lose that right, we lose every right.

* * *

MAY 23—CLAIM OF NEGROES TO FOUR FREEDOMS URGED

A speech made by one Rev. Stephen H. Fritchman to the Civil Liberties Union of Massachusetts, in which he declares that the four million Negroes in seven Southern States deserve equality and civil liberty. Imagine that! He probably has poor white folks in his own back yard, who do not know what civil liberty means, but he gazes right over their heads at the plight of Negroes singing in the corn fields a thousand miles away. It is doubtful whether the Rev. Fritchman knows what civil liberty is, himself.

* * *

MAY 27—URGE CARE IN PEACE PLANS

Former President Herbert Hoover declares that Americans must not delude themselves into thinking that fast methods of travel and communication are going to create a world-wide political and social revolution. He says, "However beguiling the thought may be, the world has not turned into a great melting pot. And we shall not achieve lasting peace by starting with the assumption that we have been transformed into one world by radio and airplanes, for if that were true, we should have no problem in making lasting peace."

Boy! Doesn't that sound like good old common sense is at long last coming through! Maybe Mr. Hoover is the man for our next President, since no other better man has appeared, and since he knows better now than to make the mistakes he made the last time.

* * *

MAY 28—JIM CROWISM ENDED AT LAST IN CHILD-CARE INSTITUTIONS

There it is again. This news-note relates how seventy-one Negro children have been accepted by institutions which have never admitted them before. They are going to mix them up with white children—in New York, of course.

* * *

MAY 28—F.D.R. ACTS TO END WAR JOB DISCRIMINATION

The President's famous FEPC died a natural death, so now he is creating a new agency to force white people to hire Negroes for war work, regardless of whether or not they have separate toilet facilities for them. Why can't these Negroes be sent to the farms, where they do not need to be skilled to help win this war? There is nothing so much needed as food at this time.

* * *

MAY 28—PRESIDENT OF LIBERIA VISITS CAPITAL

Liberia, the Negro republic, was established in 1847 to provide a home for freed slaves from America. A government patterned after our own was set up. White men are not allowed to vote. For a time it was regarded by other nations as a United States protectorate. Like a child who remembers only the bad word spoken in a conversation, the Liberians were found practicing slavery themselves by the League of Nations in 1931. Out of a population of 1,500,000 only about 100,000 along the coast are civilized. Tribal customs and barbaric practices still prevail in the hinterland, where, in 1936, an outbreak of terrorism resulted from several killings attributed to the "leopard men" of the dark interior. Only 15,000 of the present population are descendants of the original slave settlers.

Now, can anyone, possessing this information, tell me why we have to make love to the people of Liberia? The foolish things our leaders do is enough to make us tear our hair out by the roots in indignation.

Edwin Barclay, the President of this tiny Negro republic, told a press conference in Washington that their law which permits only Negroes to vote in election is a realistic one, since white men might come in and get control. This would lead one to believe that they have more sense than we do, since we permit Negroes to vote here, and had they the numbers they would soon get control, what with their aggressiveness and everything. We shall soon have to become as realistic as they are.

* * *

JUNE 21—DETROIT RIOT INJURES 200

Everyone is acquainted with this story.

The Committee which investigated the causes declared that the Negroes themselves brought it on by their insolence and lack of respect for white defense workers.

* * *

JUNE 22—TWO NEGROES HELD AFTER BRAWL IN SPRINGFIELD (MASS.)

More of the same thing.

* * *

JUNE 22—ARMY RESTORES ORDER IN DETROIT

Even dictators can subdue the uprising of a people by turning the army on them, but in time the majority will have its way. An army of blacks kept the white people of the South in subjection for a while, but when the white people had time to organize they disarmed these so-called black Union forces almost overnight. What cared that great people whether they were Federal forces or not? They knew that the National Government had gone insane. The officials in Washington are elected by the majority, and if that majority wishes to preserve itself from certain destruction those officials should do their bidding. Officials are never elected by the majority to do the bidding of any minority group.

* * *

JUNE 25—PROGRAM FOR RACIAL PEACE

A plea for whites and blacks to get along together. The white people of the South had that worked out all right until lately, when certain organizations started prodding the Negro to demand the right to enter white society. Now it appears that the Negro and white will have to part company. Destroying the white race is not the way to settle the race question.

* * *

JUNE 25—NEGROES AND WHITES WORK IN HARMONY

This shows three pictures of whites and blacks working together in a factory in New York. If the whole country had sunk to the levels of New York, we could kiss the white race good-bye. And the strange thing about it is the fact that Representatives from that State are attempting to force their low-down policies on the great South and West. God forbid it!

* * *

JUNE 25—COUNCIL TAKES STEPS TO AVERT RACE OUTBREAKS

This makes one laugh. The Honorable City Council of New York City won't strike at the root of the trouble and make a No Man's Land between the black belts and the white neighborhoods. They'll appeal to the white people to just let the Negroes have their own way, even to permitting them to buy-in in the heart of a white neighborhood.

Fortunately something rebels in a white man's breast, and he does not listen to these fallacious arguments.

AUGUST 23—RACES FIND HARMONY AT BRONX HOUSE

These places are hives of iniquity. They are established for children without regard to race and color. One such establishment in Roxbury, Massachusetts, produced such harmony between black and whites that a white girl went the whole way and married a Negro. Wonder how she felt when sex had been satisfied and she woke up to find herself ostracized from white society?

* * *

SEPT. 19—HARLEM RIOT INVESTIGATION BRINGS TEN-POINT PROGRAM

Well, it happened in spite of that "program" of the City Council. The North, pretending for over two hundred years to give the Negro equality, just naturally had that queerest of riots coming to it. Not a single white person was involved. It was an explosion of pent-up feelings of promises never made good. Why? Because the majority of white people know that you cannot give the Negro social and political equality without reducing us to a nation of mongrels.

* * *

SEPT. 19—TRENTON MUST SHOW CAUSE OF JIM CROW SCHOOL

More doings of the National Association for the Advancement of Colored People! They are determined to force white people to permit their children to mingle in school with Negro children. The queer angle to this is that they expect the Negro to like the idea of going to school with white children, and then have the white children cast them aside upon graduation, which the white children have been doing for two hundred years, and will continue to do. This makes the Negroes boil over, of course. Would it not be better all around to segregate them from the start? The National Association for the Advancement of Colored People does not realize that it is annoying the "eagle" I told about in the first part of this book.

SEPT. 26—UNION FIGHTS WITH JIM CROW

The Railway Mail Association goes to court to uphold its ban on Negroes. New York has a Civil Rights Law, which is detrimental to the white race. Such laws are an abomination before the Lord.

* * *

SEPT. 27—FIFTY NEGROES FIGHT RACE BARS IN WASHINGTON'S CAFES

A group of fifty Negroes formed an organization called Race Institute of Race Relations, and went about to various white restaurants, seated themselves, and if refused service remained until the restaurant closed for the night. This was simply another kind of picketing. As there are plenty of eating places in the Negro district of Washington, one can only conclude that the Negro men in the group simply wanted the privilege of being near and watching white girls. We white men can't blame them for wanting to do that, but we see extreme danger in it.

* * *

SEPT. 28—FATHER ASKS F.D.R. TO REVIEW PRIVATE LEVY'S CONVICTION

Boy, would the Negroes like a dictator if he happened to be on their side! The left-wing press has talked and talked about the conviction of this Negro by an Army court martial, and is attempting to get the decision set aside. Never has such an uproar been made about the court martial of a white soldier. The Army must not lose its power to handle its own delinquents, or we are in for civil war.

The President must not butt in about Levy. He will have to take his medicine, the same as all other soldiers who violate the rules and regulations around an Army camp.

OCT. 4—HILLBURN PARENTS REVEAL NEIGHBORS' "SHARE JAIL" OFFER

Another fight to get white and Negro children into the same school in a little town in New York State. There is a Negro school, but the Negroes got smart and refused to let their children attend it.

Instead, they sent them to the white school every day for a while, and after they had been refused admittance several times the parents kept them at home, in violation of the State law for compulsory attendance. The authorities threatened to jail the parents, but, believe it or not, the Negroes finally won out, and now, by the order of State Education Commissioner Stoddard, the few white children of the town have to go to school with an overwhelming number of Negroes.

This is a shame on New York State. I have watched the papers every day, hoping to see that the white parents had refused to send their children to school under such conditions. It appears that only the Negroes have the nerve to violate the laws. Too bad that those white parents have no backbone whatever.

Still, you can't blame them too much, for as I've said before, cheap, rotten literature has probably brought them to the conclusion that the Negroes are better than they are. The City of New York, being rotten to the core with radicals and communists, is forcing all the small, decent towns to follow its degrading policies down to the slough of human despond.

* * *

OCT. 2—"WARNING" AGAINST HATE-RUMORS

Decent white citizens who attempted to persuade parents of white pupils to remove their children from the school "whence Jim Crow had been kicked out" were labelled here as hate-mongers and promoters of trouble between the races.

OCT. 4—RACE HATRED CALLED CRIME

The Massachusetts Department of the Jewish War Veterans drew up a resolution declaring that race, color, or religious hatred is a crime against the Nation. They intend to seek severe penalties through the Congress and State Legislature against those promoting race hatred. Isn't that something!

A few good laws along that line, and only a complete revolution would save the white race. One would have to seize control of the Army and Navy to get anything accomplished. Still, no one wants to promote race hatred. The most one wants to accomplish is to preserve his own race.

* * *

OCT. 5—JAPS "UNCIVILIZED" IN AVIATION MURDER

President Roosevelt denounces the Japs and calls them uncivilized. He adds that he does not care very much if he does offend their feelings. Well, I'm glad he said it!

* * *

OCT. 29—NEGROES ASSAIL RULING ON F.D.R.'S RACE BIAS ORDER

Negro organizations charge that Comptroller General Lindsay Warren is "unfit and prejudiced" and call the former North Carolina Congressman's record discriminatory against the Negroes.

As Chairman of the House Committee on Accounts, Warren "bluntly refused, and boasted of refusing, to permit American citizens because of their color to patronize the public restaurant in the House of Representatives."

Warren ruled that the FEPC order, guaranteeing against racial discrimination, is not an order but a directive, and therefore that compliance is voluntary, not mandatory.

CHAPTER SIX | 133

OCT. 30—NEW PROTESTS OVER FEPC

The FEPC carried to Attorney General Francis Biddle the fight to prevent Southern Democrats from extracting the teeth from the President's order forbidding racial discrimination by firms doing business with the Government. Malcolm Ross, FEPC Chairman, admitted that doubt had been cast upon the powers and duties of the FEPC.

* * *

OCT. 29—NEGRO MADE SOLE ISSUE IN DETROIT CAMPAIGN

In the Detroit mayoralty campaign, both white and Negro voters joined forces against Mayor Jeffries because of his insistence that Negroes live in a Federal housing project along with white people, which led to the riots of Feb. 28, 1942.

* * *

OCT. 30—DETROIT WHITES WANT NEGROES BARRED

White residents of Inkster, a village bordering Detroit, petition their county board of supervisors for permission to secede from the town. The reason, Inkster will shortly receive an additional 500 Negro families in the new George Washington Carver Housing Development, a Federal project. This means that the political "balance of power" in this village, which has lived peacefully heretofore, would shift from its present white domination. The petition is opposed by the Negro populace and by a bi-racial committee.

* * *

OCT. 31—FEAR BLANKETS DETROIT AS CITY GOES TO POLLS

Campaign statements of candidates in which both agreed that they were opposed to bi-racial housing were reprinted in an attempt to split the Negro vote. The attempt of white residents of Inkster to secede because of a threatened influx of Negroes was forestalled by an injunction issued to the United Automobile Workers, a CIO local, and to the National Association for the Advancement of Colored People. More government by injunction!

OCT. 31—DETROIT SETTLES BACK

Jeffries was re-elected, in spite of votes for his opponent from working-class Negro districts.

* * *

OCT. 31—FIGHT OFF RISING STORM OF RACISM

"A storm is rising in this country. A dreadful storm, and possibly dangerous beyond anything that any one of us can foresee at the moment."

* * *

OCT. 31—"THE RACE QUESTION AND THE NEGRO"

In this book a Catholic priest, Father John La Farge, advocates "full equality" of Negroes with whites. What would become of his church if the bars were let down that safeguard the foundations of civilization and morality?

* * *

NOV. 2—SENATORS PUSH FOR AGREEMENT TO BAR "RACE HATRED" IN 1944 CAMPAIGN

Senator Guy M. Gillette, of Iowa, and Senator Warren Barbour, of New Jersey, propose an office in the Department of the Interior to investigate "hate-propaganda" and to require disclosure of identity of all issuing poltical handbills.

* * *

NOV. 2—"RISING STORM OF RACISM"

A letter from a reader of a New York paper states, "I have never seen such a pronounced feeling of racial and religious hatred among the populace as in the past few years."

* * *

NOV. 19—ANTI-SEMITIC TRACTS PRINTED IN NAVY YARD

If the Jews are not liked, whose fault is it? And who should mend their ways?

NOV. 21—SCHOOL TEXTBOOKS THAT STIR UP RACIAL HATE URGED REVISED

See it! If they can't change us they are going to change our children, whether we like it or not.

* * *

NOV. 22—SCHOOLS BEGIN RACIAL AMITY ESSAY WRITING

More of the same.

* * *

NOV. 23—RACIAL STUDY URGED IN MASSACHUSETTS

There it is. They want to teach us how to give up our race and make this a mulatto country. That's too easy. We don't need to be taught how to lay down and give up.

* * *

NOV. 24—PLAN TO FIGHT RACE HATRED IS OFFERED

Let those who wish to be loved conduct themselves in a manner inviting love.

* * *

NOV. 26—CHILDBIRTH HITS SCHOOLS

Wouldn't you expect it? With the state the country has been reduced to in morale what it is, we can only hope that the white girls are having white children. The item says that girls from 13 to 15 are being excused from classes to have their babies. Let States put the law back into the parents' hands for the handling of their children and this disgusting business will cease.

* * *

DEC. 2—DADDY OF TWELVE INDUCTED INTO ARMY

This item says that one Perry Booker, a Negro, was inducted into the army at Camp Shelby, Mississippi. He has twelve children and his family will receive an allotment of $320.00 per month. He was a porter. Holy smoke! Who said we ought to hold back inflation in this war? Down there it costs very little to live. Booker's wife ought to be able to save enough for him to buy himself a yacht when he returns. The writer's father was in the last war, and after his mother wrote to Newton D. Baker, the then Secretary of War, the family received a check for the grand total of (it was so odd a figure I remember it easily) $333.33. That was all the family of eight children ever received.

* * *

DEC. 21—DORCHESTER (MASS.) MOTHER RAPED BY TWO NEGROES

There it is again, and a fine Christmas present for Mrs. Dorothy Dunn's family. The item, spread across the front page of the boldest paper in Boston, quotes Mrs. Dunn as saying that the two Negro men followed her in a stolen car. They had observed her as she was riding along in a street car, and when she got off they pulled up alongside and seized her. In the struggle she lost her bundles and shoes. Just imagine her terror. A white girl seldom comes out of a rape alive. She had the presence of mind to pick up a social security card from the floor of the automobile as they raped her four times.

Under threat of certain death she and her husband later gave the card to the police, and the Negroes are now on the inside looking out. See what our women's beautiful skin does to the minds of men. Those two were willing to risk their very lives to clutch it for a few moments.

* * *

DEC. 22—CALEDONIA CHIEF HITS CONDUCT OF UNITED STATES TROOPS

This news has just arrived. It is a story of how U.S. Negro soldiers are misbehaving toward white women in New Caledonia. It is datelined Noumea, New Caledonia, and says that Negro soldiers from the United States were sharply criticized by Governor Christian Laigret.

He said: "Your colored problem in the States is a very difficult one and what an example your colored troops are to the colored population of this island. The colored troops are the terror of the white women of New Caledonia. They have attacked them even in the company of their husbands and brothers. Our women are afraid to go out of the house after nightfall, though recently Gen. Lincoln took action and the situation is a bit better. I have asked that the City of Noumea be declared out of bounds for your colored troops."

There now! Your writer knew that this was going to happen. It is a crime against our white family to send Negro troops into white countries when we occupy them. It is as bad as old Thaddeus Stevens did to the South after the Civil War.

What burns one up is for our newspapers to refer to the Negro soldiers as Americans, or even as Yanks. They are neither, and it is about time that we acknowledged the fact. We might call them U.S. citizens if we must call them something.

* * *

DEC. 24—ANTI-RACIAL LIBEL CASE THROWN OUT

It says that Judge John G. Brackett in municipal court found "no probable cause" against the Rapid Service Press, Inc., of Boston charged with criminal libel in the alleged publication of anti-Semitic literature.

Hurrah! For our side. They get laws put on the books, but good judges won't enforce them.

* * *

JAN. 16—JAIL SOFTENS 55 WHO SCORNED BAIL

This happened in Butler County, Missouri. Fifty-five farmers were indicted for inciting to riot. They had forcibly ejected four Negro families who had moved right into a white rural community, and had made a mass protest against the indictment by refusing to post bonds for their own release. The item says that Sheriff M. L. Hogg had only eighteen blankets for the whole group, but adds that the farmers did not need them, however, for they sat up all night telling stories, and singing songs with the jail's eight permanent residents. After one night in they decided to post the bonds and get back to their families.

* * *

FEB. 17—FREES 5 KU KLUXERS; LASHES INTOLERANCE

Five members of the KKK were freed on charges of conspiracy against racial and religious groups in Pittsburgh, Pa., by Judge Marshall Thompson on the ground that if he found them guilty he would be abridging their right of free speech. He said:

> The judges in this court include two Roman Catholics, two Protestants and one Jew, and I feel that I speak for all of them in what I am saying. If the purposes of the Ku Klux Klan are to stir up religious dissensions or racial difficulties, there could be nothing more disturbing in a country like this where we have so many races drawn from so many parts of the world, and where we have so many creeds. But while our constitution grants freedom of speech, this is a privilege which shall not be abused.

Well, now! Would the good judge consider a man speaking out to save his own race an abuse of free speech? I think not . . . not after he was made to understand just what threatens us here now. The Ku Klux Klan does not need to "go after" the Catholics or the Jews. We can absorb them both during the next few hundred years. Our great majority is bound to win by absorption. Catholic and Jewish men are marrying our daughters, and we are producing more and more beautiful daughters for their sons to marry in the future. Their offspring is slightly different from them in mind, and as Protestantism is very appealing in its liberalism it is bound to win over converts every day.

Since Christianity covers the Earth, the Jews cannot expect us to forsake it and embrace Judaism, so they may as well join us and embrace Christianity, and accept Jesus Christ as the Savior of mankind. Even today they take a great part in our celebration of Christmas, and some of them have embraced Christianity.

While on this subject, I want to say to the Ku Kluxers, that the Catholic Church is a powerful organization for good in this war torn world. Having observed Catholic children in their homes; in the streets, and on their way to and from church, I am qualified to state that they are looked after far better than our own Protestant children. Their church is constantly after their parents to bring them up right, and it does one's heart good to see how well those parents follow the church's teaching.

But here is what I like most about the Catholics. While there may be minor exceptions, which hardly matter, I do not believe they mix Negroes in with white children.

I have made it my business, here in Boston, which has a heavier Catholic population than any other city in this country, to note closely whether or not they do mix them, and I am convinced, after twenty years, that they do not. Now, there, you Kluxers; you are after an organization which is carrying your torch for you, and doing it much better than you can do it yourselves. I must add, however, that if they ever do start mixing them, I will be with you, and not with them.

* * *

MARCH 1—SOUTH CAROLINA DRAWS UP RESOLUTION

The House of Representatives in Columbia, S. C., drew up a resolution re-affirming its belief in "White Supremacy" and the majority voted it. Here is part of it:

"We indignantly and vehemently denounce the intentions, utterances and actions of any person or persons and of all organizations seeking the amalgamation of the white and Negro races by a co-mingling of the races upon any basis of equality, as being destructive of the identity and characteristics and integrity of both races.

"We reaffirm our belief in and our allegiance to established White Supremacy as now prevailing in the South . . . *and we solemnly pledge our lives and our sacred honor to maintaining it.*"

The British stock in South Carolina has been the least polluted of any in the United States. And in the above resolution you see it coming through. Men like that can't be licked. They'll never be dissolved!

* * *

MARCH 23—SOUTH MUST TIGHTEN COLOR LINE

Senator Theodore G. Bilbo of Mississippi made a speech at a meeting of the Senate of that State in Jackson, in which he warned the legislators that the South must draw the color line even more tightly. He said, in part:

> The race situation has for some time been tense in Washington. Negroes already compose 30 to 40 per cent of the population of OUR Capital city, and efforts are made by their leaders to get as many Negroes as possible on OUR Government payroll.
>
> Northerners may lightly dismiss instances of social equality practiced by them as of no serious consequence. This the South cannot do . . . Instead of understanding and help there is systematic warfare being waged in many quarters against Southern traditions and customs. We are outvoted in Congress; thus we cannot look for help from the Federal Government. . . . We people of the South must draw the color line tighter and tighter and any white man

or woman who dares cross that color line must be promptly and forever ostracized.

The superior ability of the white race has been proven both craniologically and by 6000 years of planet-wide experimentation . . . If you do not accept this as true, then you brand as false both history and biology. The white race is the custodian of the gospel of Jesus Christ . . . Anyone who would in the name of Christianity make us a mulatto people betrays his religion and his race.

When this war is over, and the 2,000,000 Negro soldiers whose minds have been filled and poisoned with political and social equality stuff return and HELL BREAKS LOOSE all over this country, I think I'll get more help in settling the Negroes in Africa. Are our soldiers and sailors fighting to save this nation, or are they fighting so that THIS WILL BECOME A MULATTO COUNTRY?

Just imagine it! While the Negroes only compose ten per cent of our population, they compose more than thirty per cent of the population of our legislative city. Smart, aren't they? The danger in this trend must be obvious to any thinking man or woman. What is the matter with us, anyway?

Sometimes I am inclined to think that if providence wasn't looking out for us there would not be one white person left in the world today. How have we survived so long?

The obvious trouble with most southern people is that they will not see that the Yankee does not really love the Negro, and that when a Yankee talks of equality for the Negro he does not mean in the North, but only in the South.

The truth of the whole matter, as I see it, after twenty years in Boston, is that a decent, respectable white northern man despises the Negro, and considers even a touch of him pollution. If this is not so why do the northern white men ban them from their hotels and apartment buildings, and insulate themselves from them by living in white communities well insulated by distance from any Negro section?

And any decent, sensible white northerner knows that if he called a Negro doctor for his daughters he would be inviting a rape and tragedy in his home. Our daughters' lovely skin simply drives a Negro out of his mind.

* * *

MARCH 24—WHITE GIRL DIVORCES SECOND CHINESE HUSBAND

This is one of those sordid stories which we all would rather not know about. A twenty-two year old white girl from Oldtown, Maine, had been divorced from her first Chinese husband in Bangor, Maine, when she was only fourteen years old. Now she is seeking a divorce from her second Chinese husband on grounds of unfaithfulness.

Think of it. A white girl seeking a divorce from a Chinese on grounds of unfaithfulness. Hadn't her parents or somebody ever told her that the code of the Orientals and other colored peoples differ greatly from that of the white man?

Here's what Gilberta Adrianne Yee told the court: "After we had been married a while, he told me I had better go back to Maine because he had another girl friend. I did, and then I got a letter asking me to come back. When I did, I found him living with another WHITE woman in our apartment. She said she was going to have a child by him, and that he must decide which of us he wanted."

Are you sick yet, Reader? The woman later threatened to kill Gilberta unless she got out of the house, and Gilberta got out. A police record was introduced showing that this Chinaman had formerly been arrested for lewd and lascivious conduct, found guilty; given a six-month sentence, and placed on probation for two years.

Gilberta testified that she had had a child by this Chinaman and that she had named him Reginald Lucien Chonney, after "a fellow in Maine" to spite her then husband, although it was his child. She got the divorce.

Before this war there was a law in Austria that a Chinaman could not employ a white woman under forty. And here in our supposedly intellectual country we still allow a Chinese laundryman to hire our girls when they are still in the bobby-sox stage, knowing full well that though white men generally refrain from putting their hands on the wrong places on our young girls, Chinamen do it without a thought of the girls' families. Let's make it a Federal law that forty is the age. A woman is wise by that time.

It is hard to understand the people of the State of Maine. If you read Senator Douglas' speech in the first part of this book, you will recall that Maine couldn't hurry fast enough to give the Negro the right to vote after the Civil War, and also give him the right to hold public office.

Now look at Maine's record for immorality, and the generally demoralized condition of her people. The case above is one, and here are two more:

A few years ago a father of a fourteen-year-old girl and her lover were arrested in Paris, Maine, for the murder of a Dr. Littlefield and his wife. A letter was found during a search for evidence of complicity that the lover had written to the fourteen-year-old daughter.

In that letter the lover had asked forgiveness for inducing the girl the night before to "go the limit" with him. Another letter which she had written him was found in which she explained that it was old stuff with her as her own father had introduced her to this business three years before.

Here's the third case:

From a woman I know to be truthful, whose relatives live in a town in Maine, I learned that a minister of said town has been very vigorous in preaching the doctrine of the equality of the white and colored races. Recently, when Negro troops moved in on them, he encouraged his own daughter to treat them as equals. She did, and one day confided to her father that she was going to have a colored baby. The whole town got the news, and it became a regular scandal. So what? That minister got up on the pulpit the following Sunday and defended her right to have a colored baby. . . . What is wrong with Maine?

* * *

MARCH 26—FIVE TO DIE FOR ATTACK ON WHITE GIRL

There it is again, only worse!

This news item, datelined Townsville, Australia, says that a white American Red Cross worker stopped a truck with five American Negroes in it and asked for a ride. She got a ride all right, for the five of them took her to a lonely spot and nearly rode her to death. She later reported the mass-rape to the military authorities, and now the men are going to die for their crime.

Now here's a question. Hadn't anyone ever told this white girl that white girls are not to be left alone with Negro men? Why, she's lucky to be alive! Perhaps she was one of those foolish white girls who would not listen to anyone, knew it all, and declared that she was not afraid of Negro men. If such was the case, boy, she had it coming to her . . . and she got it!

The above case gives me an idea for a stage or moving picture play. Let's suppose that the Negroes and communists had their way and, sure enough, our Navy started having mixed crews on ships. Now let's have the ship wrecked by a German submarine, away out in the middle of the Atlantic, and it so happens that when the

CHAPTER SIX | 145

smoke clears away we find in one lone lifeboat, two white men, six Negro men, . . . and two white women (nurses).

How does that shape up? What do you suppose is going to happen to those two white men . . . and after that to the two white women?

Every damn one of us knows the answer. Any playwright is at liberty to use this situation as a basis for a thriller, and let him try and save the white men and women in the lifeboat.

* * *

MARCH 27—NEGRO MURDERS TWO SMALL WHITE GIRLS

This happened near the village of Alcolu, South Carolina.

George Junius, a big fourteen-year-old Negro, atacked and killed, with a lead pipe, two small white girls; June Binnicker, 11, and Mary Emma Thames, 7. Dr. R. F. Baker reported that an autopsy indicated that June may have been raped. The Negro admitted the killings, but denied that he had raped either. He was rushed to the jail at Columbia to protect him from an enraged countryside.

These little girls' lives had to be sacrificed because we, damned fools that we are, will not face the truth, and put the Negroes out from among us. By the time you read this other white girls will have sacrificed their lives for the same reason.

* * *

APRIL 1—MRS. ROOSEVELT WOULD VOTE FOR NEGRO

In answer to a question from the *Ladies' Home Journal*, Mrs. Eleanor Roosevelt said that she thinks that only the qualifications of the man should be considered. What does this mean? It means that she would just as soon have a Chinaman for president, if he suited her peculiar ideas as to what kind of qualifications are desirable in a president of these United States. Not a word about safeguarding the white race. I tell you, folks, we are certainly in a bad way, and the whole world is in a bad way.

A few days ago, on a very small matter, which was equality of pay for men and women teachers in England, Mr. Winston Churchill threatened to resign his post. Just imagine it, the man we are all depending on to keep good old England from going completely communist threatening to resign. Why, I really think that all of us have been under the impression that we were helping out over there as much for Mr. Churchill's sake as for the sake of England itself. From what one can gather from the news it is quite obvious that France is on the verge of communism, as some of her best citizens are being shot for being against communism, and are called Fascists.

The same is true of Italy. The King and Marshal Badoglio are being attacked by a communist crowd there where we are established, and are called Fascists. What we want to do over here is outlaw all communists in this country as destructive of our philosophy of life.

Our best families must not be murdered. Remember Russia!

* * *

APRIL 3—SUPREME COURT GIVES NEGROES VOTING RIGHT IN TEXAS

Well, believe it or not . . . there it is. I've been afraid this would happen. What will we do now? Those Justices are appointed for life, and this decision by eight of them would, on the first blush, seem to sound our death-knell.

This case was brought by the *National Association for the Extinction of White People* for one Lonnie E. Smith, a Houston, Texas, Negro, who was excluded from voting in the 1940 primary by the election judges of the 48th precinct of Harris County.

Nine years ago the same High Court ruled just the reverse on this question of the Negroes being allowed to vote in the Southern White primaries, and it would now appear that, since the communists cannot get the poll tax abolished they have adopted this

CHAPTER SIX | 147

Inside the halls of the Supreme Court in Washington, D.C. have emerged some of the most ridiculous anti-white judicial rulings imaginable. Today the court is packed with justices who deem it necessary to rewrite the laws of the United States to favor minorities and homosexuals, and not the majority race and culture of the U.S.

---

method of accomplishing the same purpose, i.e., the putting of the Negroes over the white people of the South.

Reaction was prompt. Said Representative West, of Texas: "I don't think the Supreme Court has any more right to say who can vote in a primary than it has a right to say who can belong to a church or a lodge."

Imagine those learned Justices not realizing that giving the Negro the right to vote in a White country is giving them the right to destroy the white people. Let's hope the great men of the South can think of something. Unless they do, it is going to lead to a very serious situation, a situation which might lead to the complete breakdown of law and order in this country, and we can thank God that

Negroes do not yet run our Army, Navy, and police forces. I have an uneasy feeling that we are approaching a crisis in our internal domestic relations, and I can only hope that the good old decent American stock will assert itself and come out in complete control. After that we should form the ALL-WHITE ALL-AMERICAN PARTY and never again permit communists to exist in this great country. Destroy or be destroyed!

There should be an investigation of how the 15th Amendment got put into our Constitution, who was behind it, and how many Congressmen voted on it. I believe that our forefathers would never have established a Constitution which would in the end lead to the complete destruction of their descendants. To guard us against this they made a provision in it so that we could alter it as we saw fit to change it for our own good. Brethren, that time has now arisen! Let's cancel out the 15th Amendment by another Amendment. Any white man who votes to the contrary will be openly advocating and sanctioning the end of his own family, which is the white race. His electors could vote him out of office the next time.

Democracy, which the radicals are always shouting so loudly about, was never established here by our forefathers for the purpose of finishing off the white race. Any man who can see beyond his nose must realize that to give the vote to an aggressive people like the Negroes are is to give away our own right to say who will rule us. Lambs being nice to tigers would be no more foolish than that.

Justice Owen J. Roberts was the only Justice who dissented from the opinion giving the Negroes the vote in Texas. He was quite disgusted and bitter about it. Pointing out that the previous contrary decision given nine years before in the case of Grovey vs. Townsend, the Court had ruled that the Texas White Primary-was the same as a private club, and could bar anyone it wished to from voting in it. He said further that at that time the vote was unanimous, and that

CHAPTER SIX | 149

the present Court's policy of over-ruling previous decisions "indicates an intolerance for what those who have composed this Court in the past have conscientiously and deliberately concluded, and involves an assumption that knowledge and wisdom reside in us which was denied to our predecessors. The reason for my concern is that the instant decision, over-ruling that announced about nine years ago, tends to bring adjudications of this tribunal into the same class as a restricted railroad ticket, good for this day and train only. I have no assurance, in view of current decisions, that the opinion announced today may not shortly be repudiated and over-ruled by Justices who deem they have new light on the subject. In an era marked by doubt and confusion this Court should not itself become the breeder of fresh doubt and confusion in the public mind as to the stability of our institutions."

Said Representative Patton, Democrat, Texas: "I have an abiding faith in the great Democratic hordes of Texas that they will control their primaries and that Negroes will not vote in the white primaries. Let the Negroes form their own primaries if they like. I don't think many Negroes want to vote in the Texas white primaries. A few hot-heads are stirring this thing up. I think the Southern white man is the best friend the Negroes have."

Chairman Herbert Holmes, of the Mississippi Democratic Executive Committee, declared: "We still have a few State's rights left, and one of our rights is to have democratic primaries, and say who shall vote in them. The Supreme Court or no one else can control a democratic primary in Mississippi."

But just look how quickly the Negroes themselves were to get every white man arrested who would defy that decision. Their great Association immediately sent a letter to Attorney General Francis Biddle, demanding FEDERAL prosecution of anyone who attempted to interfere with a Negro who desired to cast a vote. Here's part of the letter: "Now that there can be no doubt that such exclusion is a FEDERAL crime, we urge you to issue definite instructions to all U.S. Attorneys, pointing out to them the effect of these decisions and further instructing them to take definitive action in EACH instance of the refusal to permit qualified Negro electors to vote in primary elections in STATES coming within the purview of the two decisions."

See it? They want the Federal Government to walk right over the States and allow them to crush the white people. Boys, the showdown is at hand. Pretty soon now we are going to see what white people in this country are for the Negro and against their own family. This crisis just had to come, and here it is. A long pent up volcano is about to burst all over us. Long live the white race!

CHAPTER SEVEN

Can We Plan Our Civilization?

> For country, children, altars and hearth (*Pro patria, pro liberis, pro aris atque focis*).
>
> —*Sallust (Catiline)*

Can we rely on the law of natural selection constantly and consistently to improve our American stock, the stock about which we are certainly more concerned than any other? Our people are our business, and when we begin to neglect our own business to look out for the business of other people we know from experience what will happen to our own.

It seems reasonable to suppose that with proper instruction on infallibility of hereditary characteristics and traits, in their high school course, our young people will be more careful in selecting their future mates for the purpose of bringing children into the world.

Even now, most young people know better than to select a mate who has insanity in the family, or one whose family is known to produce an occasional freak or dwarf. Even as much as twenty years ago, the writer had sense enough to avoid marriage with a young lady whose family was suspected of a strain of imbecility. Surely the boys and girls of today are brighter than we were then, what with the radio and improved methods of instruction. However, unless they are taught something about eugenics during their high school years, they will know nothing about it, and after they are married it is too late. We must teach them that in selecting their mates they are also selecting their children.

Buck teeth beget buck teeth, and dull parents usually beget dull children. It is essential that the children be taught while they are still young and impressionable, and before they have fallen a prey to vicious propaganda. As Plato says:

> You know . . . that the beginning is the most important part of any work, especially in the case of a young and tender thing; for that is the time at which the character is being formed . . . And shall we . . . carelessly allow children to hear any casual tales which may be devised, and to receive into their minds ideas . . . the very opposite, of those which we should wish them to have when they are grown up? We cannot. Then the first thing will be to establish a censorship of the writers of fiction . . . and we will desire the mothers and nurses to tell their children the authorized (tales) only. Let them fashion the mind with such tales, even more fondly than they mold the body with their hand . . .

And Plutarch says, in like manner:

> For childhood is a tender thing, and easily wrought into any shape. Yea, and the very souls of children readily receive the, impressions of those things that are dropped

into them while they are yet but soft; but when they grow older they will as all hard things are, be more difficult to be wrought upon. And as soft wax is apt to take the stamp of the seal, so are the minds of children to receive the instructions imprinted on them at that age.

The United States can become the leading nation of the world, in the beauty and intelligence of its men and women. We are mostly a blend of the white peoples of Europe, and many of the faults in the physical and mental make-up of the original peoples have been lost in that blend. A typical American is different from any one of his original ancestors. He is not like the English, nor the Irish, nor the German, nor the Swede; but is a happy result of the fusion of all of them. Knowing this, from our knowledge of how the tribes of Europe, in the centuries of the twilight of civilization, roamed over the land, fighting and fusing, we ought to realize that there is really only one white race. There is only one race that we can be sure that our ancestors did not mix with, and that is the colored race. For that is the only race which completely obliterates any white people which mixes with it.

In order for us Americans to plan our civilization, we shall have to adopt a correct and definite policy. We ought to be able to agree that we do not want a hybrid population, like the people of some of the islands. Anyone who likes hybrids should go to the islands and never come back. A hybrid nation would not make for progress, but would retrograde steadily.

Australia has adopted an "all white" policy, which is a step in the right direction. No colored family can settle there. They may visit, and stay about a month, but that is all. Seeing the predicament in which we now find ourselves because of the lack of foresight in our ancestors probably led Australia to plan for the future.

But nothing can ever be done as long as we permit outcasts from other countries to come in and make a hodge-podge population out of our citizenry. It is quite obvious to any thinking person that were it not for the stable, upright men and women who live in our Southern, Central, and Western States we should already be in such a social mess as to render us incapable of agreeing on anything. There would be no fixed principles, and no high moral code to live by. The corruptive and degenerative forces of our large cities are too strong for the most moral of men to resist their influences permanently. And these forces are set in motion and kept alive entirely by foreigners who have never had any morals instilled into them, and who live by working on and catering to the basest desires of men.

Nearly all our present domestic difficulties are caused by these groups of foreigners in our large cities. They are a rabble-rousing crowd who live by their wits and consequently have plenty of time on their hands to stir up agitations between employers and labor. Their "miseducated" sons become radicals, and start sensational newspapers.

Then they begin attacking real American men, and in some cases get their own "punk" elected to our Congress. They start magazines of the cheap, demoralizing, leg showing variety, and induce our young girls to expose themselves in disgraceful, degrading poses. This plays up vice, and would demoralize the whole nation, if it were small; but fortunately for us, our agricultural regions, which are vast expanses of territory, do not buy such trash, and are therefore isolated from its influence. This one fact may save our nation from complete ruin by this destructive element.

Thomas Jefferson prophetically said: "When we get piled upon one another in large cities, as they are in Europe, we shall become as corrupt as they. I view great cities as pestilential to the morals, the health, and the liberties of man."

CHAPTER SEVEN | 155

Since we are getting to the point where the policies of nearly all our large cities are controlled by this unprincipled mob, it is about time that such cities should be denied a vote in national elections. This would eliminate forever the possibility of the great United States becoming a madhouse like Europe.

One good plan would be for the schools and colleges throughout the Southern, Central, and Western States to concentrate on teaching their brightest boys the affairs of government, with the understanding that they would become the leaders when they grew up. They would need to be taught aggressiveness, for these foreigners think they are smart birds, and will try to run right over a gentleman. If they could be sent to the colleges where this riff-raff hang out they would soon learn to out-shout them. And this is important, for when men meet on the Senate floor the loudest shouter usually has his way.

Another thing which the boys ought to be taught is the fact that their home college is to be more respected than some big city college which has become degenerate from admitting riff-raff. The smart boys from the big cities who have been perverted in their minds by radical teaching in Northern colleges do not deserve any respect from real American boys who hail from the Southern, Central, and Western States.

I know, for I have lived with and talked to these empty-heads who have never known any life except the streets of the city. They actually think that their kind of life is the only kind of life, and are so distorted in their thinking that they base their whole knowledge of the Japanese, for example, on what they gained from association with one of them in college. I asked one of them which was the more important, the structure of an article or the subject matter, and he replied seriously, that the structure was the more important!

In planning for our glorious future we must see that boogie-woogie and the beat of the jungle tom-tom go out of our lives forever. It is savage! It is demoralizing, and it is not for white people. Our children should not be allowed to indulge in jungle dances which our ancestors abandoned a thousand years ago.

I have pointed out that a cheap, rotten element among us is responsible for most of our domestic difficulties, one of which is the rising delinquency among our young boys and girls. Now I have here before me a case in point. It is a large advertisement from one of Boston's big daily newspapers, and is by one of the giant moving picture producers. It shows a beautiful girl sitting up in bed, with a young man looking through the keyhole at her and muttering to himself how desirable she is. This enormous display "ad" is so conspicuous that every man, woman, and child who looks at that newspaper will see it.

If that sort of thing is not demoralizing and conducive to crime, it is difficult to imagine what would be. The men responsible for it care nothing about the morals of the people of our great country. They know nothing and love nothing but the almighty dollar. Money to them is everything.

And about the demoralizing effect of an act called "strip tease," in which a woman undresses on the stage in a totally immoral manner. England has a law forbidding this performance, and it is about time we adopted such a law. It should be a Federal law, the same as the narcotic law, for narcotics are no worse than this. Some men go away from such a performance ready to commit murder to possess a woman. Narcotics have no worse effect.

Before taking my leave, I would like to say that our thinking in this country must be clarified on certain things. Recently we had what was called "I am an American Day." Now such celebrations are all right for children, but not for thinking adults. What is an American, anyway? Is he a citizen of the United States? Or is a citizen of Canada, Mexico, or any of the turbulent, government-overthrowing states of South America also an American? One might be visiting in England, for instance, and proudly state, "I am an American," only to be floored by the answer, "I know; but where are you from?"

Why wouldn't a word like Usamerican be more specific in identifying a citizen of the United States? At present we call our flag "The American Flag," but it is the flag of the United States only. There is no specific American flag, and we ought to get out of the habit, or else let our children, and the world at large, know that we consider only white citizens of the United States to be authentic Americans.

And finally a word about our Government. It is, without doubt, the best government in the world for the average man. We do not want it changed, but constantly improved, as the mind of man sees room for improvement. More ignorant and primitive peoples may need regimentation for their own good, but not an intelligent people like us.

Our citizens do not need to be looked after by their Government, for they are perfectly capable of looking out for themselves. The poor people in these United States are not jealous of the rich people, and would not think of pulling them down to their level. They agree with these words of Abraham Lincoln: "Property is the fruit of labor; property is desirable; is a positive good in the world. That some should be rich shows that others may become rich, and hence is just encouragement to industry and enterprise . . . Let not him who is houseless pull down the house of another, but let him labor diligently to build one for himself."

And they more than suspect that Ebenezer Eliot was right when he defined a Communist as "one who has yearnings for equal division of unequal earnings."

And if the communists take over, what happens? Read this and see. After the revolution in Russia the proletariat took over. The better class people were tortured and murdered, and their property either destroyed or divided up among the revolutionaries. The very low class had been taught to hate the decent people with a venom which out and out murder could hardly satiate. There were no such things as trials.

The best men in the Nation were herded like cattle and shot without mercy. Instead of communism making every man free it made every man who was not a Government officer a slave to the State, in great fear of his life if he even spoke above a whisper. This is what a controlled press brings on. If you cannot know what is going on, but you notice the next day that your neighbor has vanished, it instills fear and dread in your soul. No wonder the Russian soldiers fight . . . wouldn't you . . . if you had been convinced beforehand that you would get it from the rear if you didn't?

Friends, that is just what Russia is like today. Stalin is Lord and Master of the Russian Army, and when one man can command millions of soldiers to do his private bidding, you can imagine what chance the private citizen has of appealing for mercy and justice, much less holler about his "rights."

Stalin has today 10,000,000 to 18,000,000 Russians . . . Russians, mind you, not Germans in labor camps for what he calls political offenses, which can cover everything.

Senator Burton K. Wheeler, Democrat, of Montana has recently had inserted into the Congressional Record at the Capitol an article written by F. A. Voight, editor of the authoritative British magazine *The Nineteenth Century and After*, which is to the point.

This magazine substantially reflects the policy of the British foreign office. After discussing the traditional British policy of maintaining the necessary "balance of power" on the continent of Europe, so that Britain "cannot be dominated," the editorial continues:

CHAPTER SEVEN | 159

All other European powers are secure if the armed might of the Germans is broken and remains broken. Only Germany can threaten Russia or France—from no other power have they anything to fear. But England could be threatened by any continental great power or coalition of powers.

To the Russian, the Germans are a nation to be unmade—and then be remade and shaped to serve the Russian national resolve. The power of the Russian State has three main foundations: the N.K.V.D. (the secret police, formerly the O.G.P.U.), the armed forces, and the labor camps. The latter are an institution unique in the modern world.

They are made up of men and women (chiefly men) who have been sentenced to detention in a labor camp for some real or alleged political offense. The usual sentence is eight years. But as the sentence can be automatically renewed, the victim, has little, if any, hope of returning to his community.

Millions of Russian subjects have been deported from one part of the Soviet Union to another. There has been a mass-deportation of Ukranians to Siberia. While his domestic problems are accumulating, Stalin has succeeded in making himself the master of the Red Army.

How does that sound? Men, we must not let law and order break down in our great country. Now the communists here are trying to get our police forces to join the CIO so that we will have no protection, and no power to stop them. We must not permit our police to be organized by gangsters against us, while your money and mine pays their salaries.

If what is written above about Russia is not entirely true, it will do very little harm, and will give someone in the know a chance to refute it and set us right on just how the government of Russia is run. If what Russia stands for is honorable and above board why does she not permit our people to visit and see for themselves what is going on?

I have an item here before me published in a Boston newspaper today which states that Rep. Philip J. Philbin, Democrat, of Massachusetts, suggested in the House of Representatives in Washington that the United States stop lend-lease aid to Nations that are engaged in invading the territorial integrity and violating the political independence of the small weak nations of Europe. He said:

> These nations are being, or, we have every good reason to believe, will be communized and their population rendered subject to Marxian dicatorship of the Proletariat.
>
> According to recent dispatches, Communistic riots and demonstrations, promoted by radicals are already occuring, even in southern Italy which is at present occupied by American forces and governed, so far as this Congress knows, by American military government.
>
> The recent attempt to interfere with the sovereignty and autonomous status of Eire by economic sanctions and other forms of intimidation has served conspicuously to bring into the focus of our American public opinion grave threats that characterize present diplomatic and military policies of some of our Allies in this fateful hour.
>
> The aggressions I refer to are being executed or threatened by a power that is allied with one phase, though not the other, of our present war effort. They are made possible in part by American arms, tanks, planes, and supplies

in voluminous quantities which we have poured in a steady, unbroken stream into that country at fabulous expenses to the American taxpayer, sacrifice to American consumers and to our own war on the Japs, and considerable loss of American life.

We are in quite a mess over there, as anyone can plainly see. Let's hope we learn our lesson this time.

What everyone needs is education, and then he will see that the nature of man is such that he is not happy when everyone is held down by law, so that there is no sense in struggling for a better life for himself or his children.

I know from my own life that to be poor is not to be miserable.

Children brought up on a farm have a perfectly lovely time without bathtubs, tiles, and electric refrigerators. The old pump or well is a fond memory, and wandering in the great outdoors with no one to stop you and hand you a questionnaire certainly is more real fun than living in the city. People in the city do not realize how they are penned in, with nothing to do but entertain friends within four walls and gradually drink themselves to death. I often wonder about Negroes who come to the city from the great open spaces and settle down in a small, dingy apartment, with only the dingier streets to wander in. One can easily imagine that they come to the conclusion that it would have been better for them had their Government forbidden them to leave the rural districts.

Having been brought up among the great middle class, whose members are continually rising into the upper classes or falling into the proletariat, I feel that I am qualified to state that the people do not want our Government to fall into the hands of the proletariat. They want good, educated people to rule over them; people who have had humanitarian principles instilled into them. People who have any knowledge of the affairs of mankind know that the proletariat can never rule, but that some gangster leaders like those that control labor unions may get them under their influence, and instead of being ruled by the people we would be ruled by hoodlums.

One way our Congress can prevent this from ever happening here is to make laws preventing any labor union from having a membership of over, say, 100,000. Then include in the laws a provision that the various unions could not amalgamate. This would enable a reasonably large army to handle any uprising. Amalgamation of labor unions may well be what caused Hitler to rise to power.

Permitting labor unions to have millions of members gives them too much political power, for by bloc voting they could elect a man like Adolph himself, or Mussolini, maybe. We want to think about these things and guard ourselves from civil war later on.

Let us hang this sign in the Capitol at Washington:

Don't Let a Dictator Have His Own Way!

Let us realize that our first step in planning our future must be to set up a separate State for the Negro, and our second step, to adopt the "all white" policy. If the Republican and Democratic parties keep on treating the Negro as a sort of political dog to be lured this way or that by the party which has the most attractive bone to offer, it will eventually become necessary for some honorable white men to form a new independent party in order to do something about establishing this separate State for the Negro.

The name of this new party could be the ALL WHITE-ALL AMERICAN PARTY. Any white man who wouldn't support such a party would obviously be against his own race and for the colored race. He could be sent along with the Negroes to their own State . . . this should make him quite happy.

In order to produce a still higher type of man and woman, the "melting pot" will have to be allowed to boil down, and not be kept in an eternal flux by the constant addition of new and raw ingredients.

Once the pot boils down, and not before, we can begin to form a race which will lead the world in progress and achievement. Insanity will be eliminated, tuberculosis will disappear, and American men and women can expect to live a hundred years, free from any disease. The population will form one big family, and there will be very few laws needed, for everyone will come at last to think alike. Vice and corruption will have no place in such a civilization. Slums will not be known, and rape and murder will be rarities indeed.

Some people are continually talking and writing as if we have an industrialist class separate and apart from the laboring class in this country, when, as a matter of fact, there is no such division among our people. There are thousands of examples of former mechanics becoming industrialists, but I would just like to point with pride to Walter P. Chrysler and Henry Ford.

Who can say that any one of the thousands of mechanics now working for others will not rise to wealth and eminence tomorrow, next week or next year? One thing is certain, they all hope to. Very few of them are satisfied with their present lot, and even though the majority of them will not ever amount to much, who can say which ones won't?

This is what makes life worth living here in our grand country. Everyone has hope, and that hope is all sustaining. It is beautiful. It urges them on, and though they may never reach their goal, the striving itself lends zest to life. Our boys and girls are usually brought up with a wonderful philosophy of their own, and if they can't have everything they just grin and enjoy life just the same.

The main thing for us to do is to keep our country as it is. A sort of defeatist attitude has been instilled into us since Mr. Roosevelt entered the White House. That attitude is to the effect that poor people will always be poor people, when we know it's not true. There has been entirely too much talk about social security, as if everyone must expect to be down and out when he or she are old. Let's not make it impossible for a poor man to set up a business, by requiring all kinds of needless reports to be made out every two weeks or so. This is not fair to our own sons who may not have much education, or industrious and ambitious foreigners who want to set up a variety store or other small business, yet cannot speak very good English, much less write it. I know personally of a man in a small town who had hardly any education, and could not spell the word "thousand," but who had managed by sheer effort to make a small fortune; built the most beautiful house in town, and brought up a lovely family. I was in his office one afternoon, and he had bargained to buy a fine team of mules with gear and wagons for $1000. That is how I learned that he couldn't spell the word, and had to have one of his boys write out the check. It was an inspiration for me.

Of late there has been much talk of the powerful countries abandoning what is called "Imperialism" and permitting the small countries and Islands to rule themselves. In this matter we ought to try and get at the truth, and so I quote verbatim here a letter that was received by a New York newspaper. It is so excellent that it should be preserved for future generations. A Veteran of the First World War wrote it. Here it is:

> You . . . do not seem to realize how great are the achievements of our New Deal in the field of international politics. By Lend-lease we have kept this war going and are causing our two greatest commercial rivals, England and Germany, to destroy each other. We are acquiring the British West Indies, Canada, Australia, New

The Parthenon in Athens, Greece is one of the finest examples of architecture created by ancient whites. Its forms have been copied again and again, not only by whites, but by other races as well.

Zealand, etc., all are becoming more and more dependent on us, and will be in effect members of the American Empire. England herself has become our advanced base for the control of Europe. Our bombing planes based on England and Italy will turn European civilization into a shambles, and thus eliminate the competition. The Germans can only retaliate by further wrecking those countries, thereby helping us. As to Russia, we have only temporarily revived her. With our vast naval and air strength we can force Japan to make war on Russia and keep Russia in her place. You of course remember that

> Japan used to be England's tool for keeping Russia at bay in Asia. As we are inheriting England's Empire, it is only natural that we pick up her tools and use them in the way she did.

That sounds like the certain course of the future, as some powerful nation will be compelled to keep the small nations from one another's throats, and we seem to be the humanitarian nation to do it.

I wonder how many people in these United States have reflected on the somewhat screwy set-up in this war. Take, for instance, the alliance of Germany with Japan, when we all know that the Germans despise all colored races. Then think about China fighting Japan, when those people are so much alike you cannot tell the difference between them. It is all very confusing. It would seem that the common sense in the world today has flown out the window.

Our foreign policy is a muddle. Other countries do not know whether we are for communism or capitalism. We ought not to be the least bashful about letting other countries know that we believe in the good old policy of "let the best man win" which is private enterprise, and that we will have nothing to do with communistic countries.

CHAPTER EIGHT

A Separate State for the Negro

Though old the thought and oft exprest,
'Tis his at last who says it best.

—*James Russell Lowell*

I have here before me a published article in which it is stated that many do not consider the Negro an American, but as a sort of stateless person, who cannot be deported because he has no home state to go to.

What's wrong with his original home, Africa? As we have read from the speeches of the great Lincoln and others of our illustrious ancestors, the Negro will have to be separated from us before we can really have peace and unity in our own family. It would be a tremendous undertaking, but it can be done, and must be done. We simply cannot allow this problem to go on growing day by day, and year by year; leaving it for our posterity to cut each other's throats over. Once we do not have the Negro among us we can experiment with all sorts of things, even communism if we want to. Perhaps instead of having a set-up where nearly everyone is poor, we can inaugurate a system wherein everyone will be rich; and "every white man a king."

The Negro is no longer content to live the underdog role in our nation, and we cannot give him political and social equality without bringing about our own downfall, therefore, whether we like it or not, we have arrived at the point in our history where we've got to face this issue squarely. The fact that most white people are compelled, on account of economic conditions, to live their lives out, (and some prefer to do so) confined within the borders of one State, yes, even one county or small town, should convince anyone that this arrangement will work no hardship on the Negro. On the contrary, as Lincoln has pointed out, since the two races cannot enjoy the same benefits here, a separate State for the Negro will be the greatest blessing that race has ever had thrust upon them. It was proven then, during Lincoln's time, that we cannot depend on the Negro to do anything, himself, about it. He prefers to remain among us, even though we enslave him. You know why, and I know why.

It really seems a pity, considering the great mass of the colored people, that we cannot longer get along, but the leaders of that race are bringing about this crisis in our relations. Perhaps it is better so, for the way they multiply, and the way we are not going to multiply because of the widespread knowledge of birth-control, maybe in a few hundred years they would outnumber us, outvote us, and even exterminate us.

Always keep in mind the fact that we have something the Negro men want, and that is our beautiful women; but in this God is on our side, for even though they do manage to get one of them now and then, God does not allow her to reproduce herself. She may have babies, but they are nothing like her, and she really leaves no descendants.

This State for the Negro could be a buffer State between us and

Mexico. It would be an ideal climate for them, since they originally came from a hot climate. Then, too, they would have an outlet to the sea by way of the Gulf of Mexico. There are thirteen million of them, so we want to give them enough territory to grow and be happy. The people who would have to move out would not long regret it. Our Government could finance this great movement of a large body of people.

Here are some of the reasons why we cannot afford to wait longer to set up this separate State:

Anyone who keeps up with the news knows that in some of the heavily populated sections of our country, except in the deep South, our girls are being taught that they are no better than Negroes. What happens is the consequence of such false and debased teaching. Edgar Hoover, the Chief of the Federal Bureau of Investigation, stated only yesterday that the increase of sex offenses among our high-school girls is appalling. He also said that a certain offense for which they are being brought in is positive proof of a serious let-down in the morals of most of them.

Even Nature cries out that a pretty white girl is its supreme effort to produce a living being both beautiful and intelligent. It displays its displeasure at a union of black and white by making the offspring neither beautiful nor very intelligent. A female of such a union finds that the lovely clothes displayed in the shop windows do not blend with her dusky skin, and that every pretty color is made for pure white skins only. She finds also that her features and lips are negroid.

Now, the one thing that makes it imperative that we lose no time in establishing a State for the Negro is the great increase in the rape and murder of white girls by Negro men. The Negro himself can hardly be blamed for committing this sub-human crime. The blame is right on our shoulders. If you put wolves with lambs you cannot blame the wolves if the temptation for so choice a morsel overwhelms them, and they devour the lambs.

This is particularly true if you taunt the wolves in every way you can by baring some of the lambs' skin, and then almost put the lamb into the wolves' mouths. That we have been doing this very thing with our lovely little lambs is obvious to any thinking person. On the stage, in night clubs, in photo magazines and newspapers—yes, even on the streets—we permit and even encourage our lambs to expose their skin and other charms to the wolves. We go farther, and throw them together in employment or entertainment, where the maddening sense of touch comes into play.

Is it any wonder, then, that sometimes the temptation to seize one of the lambs becomes overpowering, and we have another rape case on our national record? The wonder, to my way of thinking, is that it does not happen more often. The fear of certain death is, of course, the restraining factor. That our family's skin is the most desirable thing on Earth is attested by the fact that so many Negroes brave certain death to possess it for so short a time. When a thing is so alluring that a man will risk losing his life to possess it for a few minutes, it is worth preserving.

During the year 1942, in New York City, a group of Negroes attacked a white fellow on the roof of an apartment building, subdued him, and then the whole gang (this newsnote says there were twelve) held and raped his sister, one behind the other. The girl was taken to a hospital in an unconscious condition.

In that same city, a big, burly Negro attacked, raped, and murdered a beautiful white girl, backstage in a theater, while the audience was being amused by the show, which served to drown her screams.

But the butcher-knife slaying of the lovely bride of one of our young Naval Ensigns in lower berth 13 on a passenger train as it sped on its way during the night through Oregon ought to convince the most obstinate that hardly a white woman in the United States is entirely safe as long as Negro men can get at them. In this case the lady had taken a separate train from the one her husband was riding on because of the overcrowded condition brought on by the war. When the Negro was caught he told a story of how he and some of the other Negro help in the kitchen car had been drinking beer and discussing the charms of the women aboard the train. He said that he especially desired the lady he later murdered. Apparently the beer put his brain right back in the jungle state, for he took a keen boning knife, went to her berth, and when she resisted him, cut her throat from ear to ear. He beat it back to the kitchen car, and pretended to be busy, giving the impression he had not even left the kitchen.

Now, white men were sleeping all around the lady, and not one of them (I can guarantee it) ever thought of raping her. White men usually have sisters and mothers, wives or sweethearts, to think about, and they reflect that they would not have such an outrageous act committed upon their own. When a white man gets this matter settled in his mind, he no longer thinks about it. When he sees or thinks about one of our especially charming girls, he does not let the idea of raping her enter his head at all. When we hear of a white man having raped a white girl we set him down as having gone insane. There's a good reason for this. A white man in his right mind can possess a white woman without resorting to brute force and thereby instigating a lynching party with himself in the leading role.

The setting up and establishment of a separate State for the Negro is the only way in which we can save him, and at the same time not drown ourselves in the process. Once the Negro is made to understand this we can depend on his co-operation. Right thinking and teaching will accomplish this. There is no need of race riots and bloody wars. Good sense is all that is required. Let's settle this matter in time, and then everybody can be happy.

Just picture to yourself for a moment, the Negroes with a large city like New York all to themselves. Wouldn't it be wonderful for them?

They love their own peculiar type of music, and could have their own publishing concerns; their own composers, and have a great time all the time. It would be interesting to visit such a place and observe them ruling themselves. Their total number here in our country is only a little more than twice the population of New York City, but look at all the noise they are making, and the trouble they are causing us because we have to segregate them. Even our dignified Congress is right now wrangling over the soldier vote because the Southern States cannot permit them to outvote the white people.

Our leaders, who are also politicians, must forget entirely about the Negro vote. They do not need it, if both sides agree not to count their votes. It has been said that the difference between a politician and a statesman is that a politician thinks and talks about elections, while a statesman thinks about and talks about the next generation. Some of our politicians ought to ponder over that for a while, and decide to be statesmen.

This setting up a separate State for the Negro is going to take time, and we cannot do it all at once, but at least we can begin to "clear the ground." However, there is one thing we can do, and that is enact a Federal law that the marriage of a white person, within the United States and its territories, to any sort of a colored person, will thereafter be a Federal offense, which will be punished by two years in jail for both parties. Can you imagine that our brilliant law makers in Washington, some years ago, made a law called the Mann Act, which makes it a Federal offense for a man to take a woman across a State line for what is considered immoral purposes, and did not make a law prohibiting the marriage of a white person with a colored person? They are worried about our morals, but are not in the least worried about our committing suicide in that manner.

The suggested law would at least maintain our race until we get around to settling the problem once and for all. When our children see a white woman with a Negro it demoralizes them.

CHAPTER NINE

Preventing Extinction

Anyone who has read the foregoing chapters should be convinced that it is not hatred of the colored race which impels the white man to exclude colored people from white society. The white man has always thought kindly of the colored peoples of the world. But the white man cannot permit his own race to become extinct, not while he has his eyes open. The great colored family of the world has no more right to demand to be permitted to enter the great white family and destroy it than the colored customers of a white butcher, finding that he has no meat, have the right to demand that he slaughter his family to satisfy their wants. The white family would be as completely destroyed in the one case as it would in the other.

The one thing which I wish to impress on every common, ordinary white man in the whole world is the fact that he is as concerned in this matter as the biggest and most important man. The ordinary white man has as much right—and it is a natural born right—to express his opinion on this subject as the King of England has. What concerns a race of people concerns every member of it, and no man or group of men has the right to make legislation affecting the whole race without first consulting its members. This is particularly true when such legislation has to do with the very survival of that race.

A man may risk his life to save that of another, but when it is obvious to him that he will positively lose his, it behooves him to think twice whether or not he may be more valuable to civilization than the man whom he would save.

For a nation to retain its decency it is necessary for the people who govern it to be honorable and respectable, therefore I would like to suggest that we make it a law throughout the country that any man who runs for public office shall, at Government expense, have his entire record published for every voter to read. This would forever deter a criminal from seeking public office. It is our duty to do this. It is for the good of our own children that we should do it. Any man who would vote against such a law can be set down as a scoundrel.

Some time ago Prime Minister Churchill stated that he had not become the Prime Minister of England to preside over the liquidation of the British Empire. It was a laudable declaration. England cannot exist without its Empire, and some people do not seem to know that India comprises four-fifths of that Empire. Cut off the body and the head will expire in very short order. It does cause one to laugh though, at the mistakes that civilized countries make. England takes Nehru, for instance, and educates him at Oxford, and what happens? The British have to throw him in jail because he knows too much.

It's a good thing the English have not educated the whole of India, or England would not be in existence today.

Coming back to our own country, it would be a great thing if

President Roosevelt came out with a statement that he had not been elected President to preside over the liquidation of the white race. His Fair Employment Practices Act, and the doings of his wife would lead one to believe that he had been elected for the specific purpose of reducing us to a mulatto nation.

The white race exists solely on the pride it takes in being white, and once a person takes no pride in being white that person is doomed to go down.

There is both good and bad news from New York today. I see that the good people of Hillburn actually withdrew the white children from their own school when it was invaded by the Negro children under the orders of School Commissioner Stoddard. This is up-to-date proof that a Government cannot force a beautiful, intelligent race into degradation.

The bad news from New York is that the assistant manager of a Times Square hotel, Martin A. Nicholas, was fined $100 for refusing to admit a Negro. This is an outrage! Why aren't the Negroes satisfied with their own hotels? I'll tell you why! They want to get near to our lovely women!

Doesn't that convince anyone that we only have to watch communistic New York to see how things will proceed if we don't soon crack down on the rotten element in these United States? And we must remember that being the most intelligent and powerful nation on this Earth that what we do the whole world will be compelled to do. We . . . today . . . are the protectors and guardians of the white race of the entire world. As time rolls on the white race must not roll into oblivion!

I know not . . . what other men may think, but as for me . . . if our lovely children and beautiful women are not worth preserving then nothing is worth preserving . . . and I would shout . . . TO HELL WITH EVERYTHING, LET THE DEVIL TAKE OVER!

But hark! As I go overboard I hear the sound of running feet . . . yes, thousands . . . wait, millions . . . of men running . . . to save . . . the child (the Race) . . . it's wonderful . . . just listen to those thundering feet . . . the child WILL be saved . . . you can't stop them . . . the clarion has sounded! Now what happens to me does not particularly matter . . . it's only the future of the race that matters. I've done my duty and service to my own family . . . which is the white race . . . and I am content, for a man who writes a good book, talks back, onward through the centuries, advising and counseling humanity from the grave.

* * *

In order to give the reader of this book an idea of the various countries of the world and their strength in populations, I hereby present a list of the important ones. Now, bear in mind, for comparison, that the City of New York alone has a population of around 7,000,000. Our country, the United States, has a total population of approximately 130,000,000. Taking out the Negro will leave us approximately 117,000,000.

IMPORTANT COUNTRIES AND THEIR POPULATIONS

Country	Government	Population (1944)
Austria-Hungary	Emperor	49,880,000
Argentina	Republic	13,518,239
Australia	British Empire	7,137,000
Belgium	Kingdom	8,386,553
Bolivia	Republic	3,426,296
Bombay	British Empire	26,347,509
Brazil	Republic	41,356,605
Bulgaria	Kingdom	6,549,664

CHAPTER NINE | 179

Canada	British Empire	1,419,896
Ceylon	British Empire	5,312,548
Chile	Republic	5,000,782
China	Republic	457,835,475
CzechoSlovakia	Republic	15,247,000
Denmark	Kingdom	3,805,000
Egypt	Kingdom	15,920,703
England	British Empire	37,920,917
Finland	Republic	3,863,753
France	Republic	41,907,056
Georgia	U.S.S.R.	3,542,289
Germany	Republic	79,375,281
Greece	Republic	7,108,814
India	British Empire	352,837,778
Ireland	British Empire	2,989,700
Ireland (Ulster)	British Empire	1,279,745
Italy	Kingdom	45,354,000
Jamaica	British Empire	1,223,241
Japan	Empire	72,875,800
Korea	Japanese	22,633,587
Latvia	U.S.S.R.	1,950,502
Liberia	Republic	1,500,000
Lithuania	U.S.S.R.	2,879,070
Luxemburg	Grand Duchy	301,000
Mexico	Republic	19,473,741
Netherlands	Kingdom	8,728,569
New Caledonia	France	53,245
Newfoundland	British Empire	300,000
New Zealand	British Empire	1,640,901
Norway	Kingdom	2,937,000
Palestine	British Mandate	1,568,664

Poland	Republic	34,775,698
Portugal	Republic	7,539,484
Rumania	Kingdom	13,291,000
Russia	Empire	182,182,600
Scotland	British Empire	4,842,980
Sicily	Italy	4,000,078
Spain	Republic	25,878,000
Sweden	Kingdom	6,406,474
Switzerland	Republic	4,260,719
Tunis	France	2,608,313
Turkey	Republic	17,869,901
Uruguay	Republic	2,146,545
Venezuela	Republic	3,492,747
Wales	British Empire	2,593,014
Yugoslavia	Kingdom	16,200,000

It will be noticed by the above statistics that Norway, Sweden, Switzerland, Finland, Denmark and a remarkable number of other countries have hardly enough population to be called countries. It is as if every one of our States were separate countries, instead of being united into one great and powerful whole. If our country was divided into all these small nations we would be continuously at war too.

When you come to think of it, Europe seems to be a hopeless case, unless some powerful nation takes all the small nations under her wing, and compels them to behave. They could be united under a central government, with each little country retaining its autonomy, but it appears that this will never be done, and the small nations be forever subject to aggression from a more powerful neighbor.

Joining hands with England, we ought to compel the nations of

CHAPTER NINE | 181

Europe to form a confederation, so that we will not be continuously sending troops over there to settle their disputes. England could rule them like she rules India's millions, and they would be better off for it. If, as has been reported, Russia has sounded the death knell of the white people in her territory by making it against the law for white people to bar Negroes from their homes under penalty of death, the white people of Europe proper would do well to get under England's grand protective wing in very fast order. One can almost hear the old British Lion letting out the loudest roar he has ever made against such amalgamation of the white and colored races.

Now just take a look at the above chart, and note the populations of Germany and Russia. The Russians have been flattered to death about their brave fight against the Germans. But look at Russia's population. She has more than twice the population of Germany from which to draw her Army. Now, who looks to have the most skill? Maybe Germany has used some troops from other countries, but we all know that the Germans would have to command and guide them.

And what about China and Japan? Let's glance at their populations. China has more than six times the population of Japan.

How can we account for China's failure to crush Japan in short order? The reason is that China is overrun with different factions, and the population is mostly made up of ignorant coolies and their families. It is astounding how a civilization can be thousands of years old, and yet not produce one man who possessed the ability and character to organize his people and lift them out of the dust. This bears out my constant preaching that a mongrel people will not make for progress, but will regress steadily unless the White man steps in and helps them. The question always will be: How far can the White man go in helping them without bringing on his own eventual obliteration, and as a consequence, the end of civilization?

One hears every now and then that what really caused the downfall of France was the demoralized condition of her people, and that this demoralization started during the First World War when thousands of Negro troops moved in. It is so disgusting that I have tried not to believe it, but still our boys who returned say that French white women fell all over the Negroes, and even married them.

This apparently spread all through France, and pretty soon the whole Nation lost any pride of race or country. When the Germans really attacked, thousands of those Frenchmen who retained an iota of decency hoped the Germans would win and save them from a regime both political and social which was leading the entire Nation into degeneracy and ruin. If the case as stated is true, then it will be up to England and the United States to set France right in this serious matter, for France is the gateway to all Europe. We must keep her strong and decent.

If the French persist in mixing with Africans, there will be no real French left, and we will have to write her post-mortem, evacuate the mulattoes out of France, and re-populate her with white people.

Europe cannot have a colored nation shoulder to shoulder with her white nations. Having Turkey, with its population of 18,000,000, where it is, is bad enough. Turkey is, oddly enough, in the same relationship to the rest of Europe, as the State I have suggested for our Negroes would be to us. The Negro State would have about the same population as Turkey.

Here is a birdseye view of Europe's size compared with the colored continents of Asia and Africa. Asia and Africa combined have a colored population of approximately 1,100,000,000. Asia and Africa combined have an area of approximately 28,800,000 square miles.

Europe, which includes the islands of England, Scotland, and Ireland, is bounded by the Ural Mountains in the East and by the Mediterranean Sea in the South. It has an over-all area of approximately only 3,872,000 square miles. The whole combined population is approximately only 500,000,000.

As the continents of Europe and Asia are touching at a comparatively small point, one might say that, as regards size, if the two continents formed a lion, Europe would be the snarling head. That is how small Europe is as compared with Asia, and we all know that Europe has long been a snarler.

Someone ought to get busy and write a history of the wars the white people of Europe have waged these thousands of years to hold back the colored races of Asia and Africa. The Turks were stopped right where they are now in 1389, but since then they have waged innumerable wars against the neighboring white countries, sometimes slaughtering thousands of Hungarians and Poles. In 1571 Spain defeated the Turks at Lepanto, and taught them a lasting lesson.

The continent of Africa has an area of approximately 11,500,000 square miles, which is more than three times the square mile area of the United States. Its population is only 150,000,000, which is about 20,000,000 more than we have. This indicates that there is plenty of room in Africa, and according to the encyclopedias she is very rich in natural resources.

Therefore, since we have demonstrated our ability to ship 10,000,000 men to Europe and Australia in very short order, why don't we do this thing right in the first place, and ship the Negro back to his original home?

Perhaps we will never again have the wonderful shipping facilities we will have immediately after this war, and this would be a constructive project which will benefit both races for thousands of years to come. White countries which hold empires in Africa should be glad to relinquish them, and help us to establish African independence there. Our Negroes could, with what they have learned from us, develop that continent in a big way.

One other thing we must do is open our gates to any white people who are being overrun by a colored race. We will need their numbers later on as sure as your children will be born white. East is East, and West is West . . . and for the good of the West may they never meet. Divided WE stand, united WE fall.

— END —

ONLY BOOK OF ITS KIND IN THE WORLD!
MARCH OF THE TITANS

Here it is: the complete and comprehensive history of the White Race, spanning 500 centuries of tumultuous events from the steppes of Russia to the African continent, to Asia, the Americas and beyond. This is their inspirational story—of vast visions, empires, achievements, triumphs against staggering odds, reckless blunders, crushing defeats and stupendous struggles. Most importantly of all, revealed in this work is the one true cause of the rise and fall of the world's greatest empires—that all civilizations rise and fall according to their racial homogeneity and nothing else—a nation can survive wars, defeats, natural catastrophes, but not racial dissolution. This is a revolutionary new view of history and of the causes of the crisis facing modern Western Civilization, which will permanently change your understanding of history, race and society. Covering every continent, every White country both ancient and modern, and then stepping back to take a global view of modern racial realities, this book not only identifies the cause of the collapse of ancient civilizations, but also applies these lessons to modern Western society. The author, Arthur Kemp, spent more than 25 years traveling over four continents, doing primary research to compile this unique book—a book to pass on from generation to generation. New deluxe softcover, signature sewn, 8.25" x 11" format, 592 pages, four-page color photo section, indexed, appendices, bibliography, chapters on every conceivable White culture group and more.

High-quality softcover, 592 pages, #464, *$42*

Available from THE BARNES REVIEW, P.O.Box 15877, Washington, D.C. 20003. TBR subscribers take 10% off. Call 1-877-773-9077 toll free to charge to major credit cards. Also see www.barnesreview.org.

RUDOLF HESS: HIS BETRAYAL & MURDER

BY ABDALLAH MELAOUHI

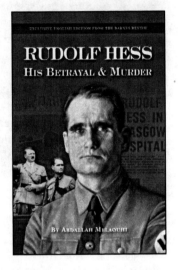

Most of you already know the story of Rudolf Hess, Hitler's right-hand man, and how he flew off to England to make peace with the British. His plane, of course, crashed in Scotland and he was made a prisoner of the Allies. Hess was immediately locked up and kept in solitary confinement nearly the rest of his life. What truths about the war did Rudolf Hess possess that were of such danger to the Allies?

As for me, I worked as a male nurse caring for Rudolf Hess from August 1, 1982 until his murder on August 17, 1987 at the Allied Military Prison in Spandau. On the day of Mr. Hess's death, I was called to the prison from my flat, which was located in the immediate vicinity of Spandau Prison. I was told that there had been "an incident."

When I entered the summerhouse, the scene was like a wrestling match had taken place. The body of Mr. Hess was lying on the floor, apparently lifeless. Near to his body stood two soldiers dressed in U.S. Army uniforms.

In my view, it is clear that he met his death by strangulation, at the hands of a third party. But when I voiced my objections, I was threatened with professional ruination—or worse. For years I kept silent. But now I have told the entire story of my time with my friend Rudolf Hess, a man of great vision, intelligence and compassion, in a new book called *Rudolf Hess: His Betrayal and Murder*.

I guarantee that every word inside is the complete truth in regard to what I know about what happened to Mr. Hess and what I learned about him as a man. Softcover, 291 pages, #643, $25 plus $5 S&H inside the U.S. from TBR, P.O. Box 15877, Washington, D.C. 20003. Call 1-877-773-9077 toll free to charge.

HITLER
𝔇emocrat

What you "know" about Adolf Hitler and his era may be nothing close to the truth!

When retired Belgian General Leon Degrelle—the last surviving major figure from World War II—died in Spain in 1994, he was in the early stages of a proposed fourteen volume series of works to be collectively titled "The Hitler Century." At the time of his death, the colorful and outspoken—and exquisitely literary—Belgian statesman had completed some three volumes, but outrageous and insidious intrigues by certain enemies of truth in history sabotaged most of his work. However, thanks to the energetic efforts of a group of honest historians—graciously supported by Madame Degrelle, the general's widow—a substantial portion of his work was rescued and published over a period of years in THE BARNES REVIEW, the bimonthly journal of Revisionist thought. Now, that material appears here in *Hitler Democrat* between two covers for the first time. In the end, this volume is not only a monumental work of history, a genuine epic, but it is also in its own fashion a tribute to the man behind it: front-lines fighting Waffen SS officer Leon Degrelle.

GEN. LEON DEGRELLE

Now, for the other side of the story, as only Leon Degrelle could tell it, read *Hitler Democrat* (Softcover, 546 pages, #622, $35 plus $5 S&H inside the U.S. Outside U.S. email sales@barnesreview.com for S&H.) To order additional copies, call 1-877-773-9077 toll free to charge or write TBR, P.O. Box 15877, Washington, D.C. 20003. See also www.barnesreview.org.

In the maverick tradition of one of the great historians of the modern era . . .

No topic is "too controversial" for THE BARNES REVIEW, the most interesting history magazine published anywhere today. Commemorating the trailblazing path of the towering 20th-century revisionist historian, the late Harry Elmer Barnes, TBR's mission is to separate historical truth from propaganda and to bring history into accord with the facts. Founded in 1994 by veteran American nationalist Willis A. Carto—a personal friend of Barnes—*The Barnes Review* concurs with Rousseau's maxim that "Falsification of history has done more to impede human development than any one thing known to mankind." TBR covers all aspects of history from the dawn of man to recent events and also places a special focus on the philosophy of nationalism. As such, TBR proudly describes itself as a "journal of nationalist thought" and dares to be politically incorrect in a day when Cultural Marxism prevails in the mass media, in academia and in day-to-day life. TBR's editorial board of advisors encompasses historians, philosophers and academics from all over the face of the planet, intellectuals united in their desire to bring peace to the world by exposing the lies and prevarications of the past that have brought us to where we are today. If you believe everything you see in the "responsible" media or think that absolutely everything that appears in most college-level history texts is true, you might be shocked by what you see in TBR—but if you are shocked by what you see in TBR, then that's all the more reason you need to join the growing ranks of independent-minded free-thinkers from all walks of life and all over the world who are longtime TBR subscribers.

Isn't it time you subscribe?

THE BARNES REVIEW $46 for ONE year (six bimonthly issues—64 pages each); including this special free bonus: A COPY OF Michael Collins Piper's *Share the Wealth: Huey Long vs Wall Street*. That's a $20 gift free for a one-year domestic subscription. Subscribe for two years at $78 and get *Share the Wealth* PLUS *Final Solution: Germany's Madagascar Plan* free. Outside the U.S. email sales@barnesreview.org for rates or see the form at the back of this book.

Call 1-877-773-9077 today and charge a subscription to major credit cards. Send your check, money order or credit card information (including expiration date) to: The Barnes Review, 645 Pennsylvania Avenue SE, #100, Washington, D.C. 20003.

CPSIA information can be obtained at www.ICGtesting.com
Printed in the USA
BVOW01s0216131114

374910BV00005B/12/P